walking
in the
wilderness

SEEKING GOD DURING LENT

BETH A. RICHARDSON

UPPER
ROOM BOOKS®
Nashville

Upper Room Books® website: upperroombooks.com

Upper Room®, Upper Room Books®, and design logos are trademarks owned by The Upper Room®, Nashville, Tennessee. All rights reserved.

Scripture quotations not otherwise marked are from the New Revised Standard Version Bible, copyright 1989 National Council of the Churches of Christ in the United States of America. Used by permission. All rights reserved.

Scripture quotations marked CEB are from the Common English Bible. Copyright © 2011 Common English Bible. Used by permission.

Cover design: Lindy Martin | Faceout Studio
Cover imagery: Stocksy
Interior design and typesetting: PerfecType | Nashville, TN

Print ISBN: 978-0-8358-1933-6 | Mobi ISBN: 978-0-8358-1934-3 | Epub ISBN: 978-0-8358-1935-0

Printed in the United States of America

To Jenni

Contents

CONTENTS

Acknowledgments

I wrote this book at a time of deep trouble in the world. I am grateful for the opportunity to speak into the wilderness through which we journey these days. Thank you to all those who walk with me, who have given me hope, support, love, and encouragement during seasons of challenge. Thank you to all the prophets who tell the truth, challenging us, reminding us that we can do better. Thank you to the healers and encouragers who pick up the broken pieces. Thank you to each person who, despite their fear, steps into the desert, following the call of the Holy One to take a stand against the forces of evil. I am grateful for your witness, your courage, and your contribution to my life and to the world.

I'm grateful to Joanna Bradley Kennedy for inviting me to write a Lenten book and for her gracious and sensitive editing of the manuscript. Many thanks to the staff of The Upper Room, the community of the Academy for Spiritual Formation #41, and the teachers and students of the Haden Institute. You are my spiritual family. You continue to love me, teach me, and mentor me in my journey as a writer, editor, spiritual director, musician, leader, and worship nerd.

And thank you to my family. To Jenni, Arya, and JJ, who fill my life with joy.

The season of Lent may be the most emotionally charged season of the Christian year. It is a forty-day journey (not counting Sundays) when we watch the tight-knit community of Jesus and the Twelve form and grow in what it means to be faithful to the loving God Jesus tenderly called Abba. Jesus confronts and overcomes temptation in the loneliness of the desert. As he faces the cost of his mission of salvation, Jesus' prayer reveals both his agony and his trust: *My Father, if it's possible, take this cup of suffering away from me. However—not what I want but what you want* (Matt. 26:39, CEB). We see in Jesus the faithfulness we desire and the trust to practice it in good times and hard times.

There is practice and there is failure as the disciples face their own temptations and as they are sent out to serve, heal, teach, and proclaim the reality of God's kingdom on earth. Lent is a time of deep reflection as we consider the desert places of our own lives and the practice and failure that meet us in our own quest for faithfulness to the God of love, peace, and justice.

—Rueben P. Job, Norman Shawchuck, and John S. Mogabgab,
A Guide to Prayer for All Who Walk with God

Introduction

Everywhere and always God is with us, near to us and in us.
But we are not always with [God], since we do not remember [God]. . . . Take upon yourself this task—to make a
habit of such recollection. Make yourself a rule always to be
with the Lord, keeping your mind in your heart, and do not
let your thoughts wander; as often as they stray, turn them
back again and keep them at home in the closet of your
heart, and delight in converse with the Lord.
— Saint Theophan the Recluse, *The Art of Prayer*

I never aspired to write a book for the Lenten season. I have always been
so much more attracted to the softness of the season of Advent—the
music, the candles, the preparation of hearts for the coming of a baby.
In fact, I may have been heard to say, "I will never write a book about
Lent." But here I am, writing a book for Lent, this season of wandering
in the wilderness. Just as we need room in our hearts during the season
of Advent—in preparation for Jesus' coming into our midst—so also
do our hearts need spaciousness to prepare for the events of Holy Week.
That infant from the Christmas story has been born, has grown up,
and has started his ministry. We follow his journey through the Lenten
scriptures. He is wandering the countryside, teaching and healing, all
with his disciples in tow. And we all know what is going to happen.
Soon, Jesus and his disciples will be walking toward Jerusalem and the
violent ending that we know is coming.

And our hearts need preparation. Since the early days of Christianity, the period preceding Easter has been observed as a season of fasting and repentance. Those forty days—excluding Sundays—are an imitation of the forty days Jesus spent in the wilderness at the beginning of his ministry. The practice of Lent was formalized by the First Council of Nicaea in 325. The early Christians observed Lent as a time of preparation for their entry into the Christian faith. Converts spent the season of Lent fasting, learning, and readying their hearts and lives for their initiation into Christianity. The ritual of baptism was performed at Easter—baptism, its own form of resurrection. The disciple is dipped under the water (the dying) and brought up out of the water as a new person (the resurrection).

During Lent today we still participate in these early Christian traditions of fasting and repentance. Many of us continue to observe a rule of no meat on Fridays. We fast from negative habits—apathy, cynicism, or judgment of self or others. We fast from chocolate or desserts or carbonated beverages or social media. Or we take on something new during Lent—a new spiritual discipline of prayer or silence, the study of a Lenten devotional guide, or the intention of keeping a Lenten art journal.

Some of this book's concepts are rooted in the desert tradition of the Christian church. In ancient times, the *abbas* and *ammas* (fathers and mothers) of Egyptian monasticism made their home in the desert, alone in hermitages or gathered in communities. Their experiences of living alone or in community, facing temptation, and learning to live in God's grace became the roots of the monastic movements of later centuries. Recountings of their experiences developed into a body of stories from the desert fathers and mothers. The concept of remembering God through the day comes from this ancient tradition. Additionally, from this tradition comes the daily element in this book: receiving a word or phrase to carry with us into the day. Pilgrims would come to the *ammas* and *abbas* and ask, "Give me a word of life." So, at the end of each day's reflection, I offer a word to carry through the day. This word can be written down in a phone or computer or written on a sticky note and placed on a refrigerator or a desk. Others may choose to pray with their cameras by taking pictures that represent the word and sharing them with friends. We come hungry to this season of Lent—hungry for words of life, for rituals of preparation, for practices to help us on our way. And this book will help us to remember God, to receive words of life, and to walk with one another through the days of Lent.

Into the Wilderness

> The Greek word traditionally translated "desert" or "wilderness" . . . doesn't mean hot and dry. It means uninhabited, lonely, with no human population. . . . Every area of life has some potential to be desert. . . . The truth is that we must simply learn to live in the desert, must try to remain oriented toward God as we go on through the misery. The divine presence is not the way *out* of the desert, it is the way *through* the desert. Remain attentive to God, stay utterly dependent on God—this is the lesson of the desert.
> —David Rensberger, *Weavings*[1]

More and more in these days of social, political, religious, and spiritual upheaval, I find myself feeling that I have entered an era of exile, wilderness, wandering through the desert. I'm not sure exactly when we arrived here. It might have been around the time that the 24/7 news cycle really got going. Or when life accelerated and we experienced information overload, our senses overwhelmed with data much of the time. Or when our earth began to groan and we could no longer ignore the effects of climate change—melting ice and rising sea levels, droughts, hurricanes, and typhoons. Or when the global crises of rampant xenophobia and overt racism made us cry out. Or when the pandemic arrived.

Phyllis Tickle, author and scholar, began writing and speaking in the 1990s about an upheaval that would be facing our church and our world. Tickle wrote, "Every five hundred years, give or take a decade or two, Western culture, along with those parts of the world that have been colonized or colonialized by it, goes through a time of enormous upheaval, a time in which essentially every part of it is reconfigured."[2] Five hundred years ago, the upheaval was the Reformation with Martin

Luther's ninety-five theses and the creation of the printing press. Tickle wrote about The Great Emergence of our years as "the Semi-Millennial Tsunami of Change" facing us right now.

I believe that the Great Emergence is the wilderness in which we are finding ourselves. It is as though one day we woke up, looked out of the window, and saw that we were in unfamiliar territory. Recognizable landmarks were gone, and we couldn't quite find a solid footing beneath us. Now, we find ourselves wondering what has happened and just how to navigate, survive, or even thrive in this wilderness. David Rensberger notes in his article in *Weavings* that periods of wilderness are inevitable for us. "In a sense," he writes, "everyone who has chosen the life of commitment to God has chosen the desert."[3] And we can know that, at some time or another, we will be, like the Israelites, like John the Baptist, like Jesus, walking in the wilderness for forty days (or forty years!).

So we enter this season of Lent—these forty days—and we enter the wilderness of Lent. One of our tasks in this season is to make space in our hearts—hearts overflowing with things that are not God. Hearts that have no room for the Holy One, for the suffering of our neighbors, for paying attention to how God is calling us to be in this time of upheaval. We begin Lent, as Sarah Parsons writes, "by seeing things we would rather not see."[4] We may see biases and fears that get in the way of our ability to provide sacred hospitality for others. We may see habits that keep us from opening our hearts to the Holy One or to neighbors in need. We may see addictions that affect our health or relationships.

Our Lenten invitation from the book of Joel says, "Yet even now, says the LORD, return to me with all your heart, with fasting, with weeping, and with mourning; rend your hearts and not your clothing. Return to the LORD, your God, for [God] is gracious and merciful, slow to anger, and abounding in steadfast love, and relents from punishing" (2:12-13).

"Rend your hearts," the prophet calls to us. Let us make space for God's Spirit, God's teaching and shaping of us, so that we might be fully present to the Holy One and to our neighbors. May we keep the eyes of our heart open to the mystery of Christ's death and resurrection; may

we make space in our heart for the miracle of the rebirth to which we
are invited.

Purpose of the Book

This book is meant to be a companion during the season of Lent. We
may be traveling in the wilderness, but we are not alone. We travel
together, holding this sacred space for one another. And the Spirit trav-
els with us into our wilderness journey.

Christian spirituality focuses on helping us remember God
throughout our day.[5] From Paul's exhorting the Thessalonians to "pray
without ceasing" (1 Thess. 5:17) to Brother Lawrence's practicing the
presence of God in each daily task, we are challenged and encouraged
to connect with God—to remember God—not just during formal worship or daily meditation time but throughout the day. Theophan the
Recluse exhorts us to remember God: "Make yourself a rule always to
be with the Lord, keeping your mind in your heart, and do not let your
thoughts wander; as often as they stray, turn them back again and keep
them at home in the closet of your heart, and delight in converse with
the Lord." We need not get discouraged if remembering God throughout the day is difficult. This practice is a skill to be developed over time,
a practice learned over a lifetime.

During the coming days, I invite you to remember God as much
as you can; in doing so, you will maintain a true center during this
holy time. Carry one of the elements from each day's reflection with
you into the day, and, at any time, take a break and remind yourself of
God's presence. Think about the Sunday's spiritual practice. Meditate
on the word for that day. Say a prayer. Or just pause and create silent
space inside yourself. Feel God's love filling you. Remember God when
you realize you are in a wilderness. Remember God when you watch the
news or observe a friend's sadness. Remember God when surrounded
by a crowd, sitting alone or isolating, or lying in bed in the quiet of
early morning. Remember God when you check your email, post on
social media, or when you receive a text message. *Remember God.* God
is there, waiting for you to remember.

Using the Book

This book may be used by an individual or a group. Each day's meditation invites the reader to stop and connect with God for that moment and then later during the day. A group study guide offers suggestions for using the book as the focal point of six Lenten gatherings. Additionally, litanies for Ash Wednesday, Holy Week, and Easter can be found at the end of the book. These litanies can be used during corporate or personal worship.

The book begins on Ash Wednesday and continues through Easter Sunday, and the days are numbered from one through forty. Sundays during Lent are not fasting days but are considered "little Easters," and these days are not included in the count to forty. On Sundays, I introduce a collection of spiritual practices that I believe we need for these times of exile and wilderness. They are being present, lament, *lectio divina*, trust, compassion, and hospitality. Whether these practices are old friends or new experiences, I hope they will sustain us in these days in the wilderness.

Each day's meditation stands on its own and contains the following items: a quote from a resource published by The Upper Room, a short scripture, a reflection and prayer written by me, and a word that evokes a theme for each day. If nothing else, I invite readers to carry the word from the day's reading with them throughout the day.

At the end of the book, you'll find a group study guide. Although you can use this resource by yourself, I encourage you to find a way to join with others during this season. The members of your supper club, Sunday school class, or a group of friends or colleagues may want to covenant with to use the book during this season. If you don't have such a group to join, I encourage you to find at least one other person who will read the book with you. In this way, you will receive and give support during your Lenten journey.

ASH WEDNESDAY

God, you have made me and you know me.
I am empty and find myself in darkness so dark
    that I am overwhelmed by its density. . . .
You alone know the thoughts that assault my mind.
You alone know my anxious ways.
You alone know the demands that haunt me unceasingly. . . .
God, where are you in all this?
You said that you would not leave me,
yet I feel abandoned and exposed.
Rescue me from me.
Quick, God, I can't wait.
Send your Spirit to my rescue, in the name of love.
Amen.

—Juanita Campbell Rasmus, *Alive Now*

Scripture

Yet even now, says the LORD,
    return to me with all your heart,
with fasting, with weeping, and with mourning;
    rend your hearts and not your clothing.
Return to the LORD, your God,

for [God] is gracious and merciful,
slow to anger, and abounding in steadfast love,
   and relents from punishing.

—Joel 2:12-13

Reflection

Today is Ash Wednesday, the beginning of Lent. On this day, we receive ashes on our foreheads in the sign of a cross, given with these words of remembrance: "From dust you came. To dust you will return."

This ritual is a reminder of our mortality, for sure. But to me, Ash Wednesday is also a reminder of our connection to all of creation. We are made of dust, and to dust we will return. Some of the particles that we are made of could have been part of a solar system that disappeared millions of years ago. I like to think I carry in my cells remnants of the red clay of southwest Oklahoma and the deep black peat of ancient Ireland.

During the season of Lent, we return from our wandering ways back to the Holy One. We take time to watch for the habits, obsessions, and actions that separate us from God. We give up something or take on something new—perhaps a prayer practice or an intention—that will help us unclutter stuffed-too-full hearts.

On this day we return to God, remembering that we are God's beloved, that we were imagined by God before we were born, and that we will be loved by the Holy One for all time.

God of ashes, you created the universe, and you created me. Remind me through today's ashes that I am your beloved. Let me walk these days of Lent remembering who I am and whose I am. Amen.

———————

Carry This Word in Your Heart Today

Return

Day 2

Lent begins in the wilderness. . . . Even against our better judgment, we must begin these forty days [of Lent] by going alone to a wild place—in ourselves or in our lives. If we are fiercely honest with ourselves as we begin a Lenten journey toward greater openness, we must start by seeing things we would rather not see.

—Sarah Parsons, *A Clearing Season*

Scripture

In those days Jesus came from Nazareth of Galilee and was baptized by John in the Jordan. And just as he was coming up out of the water, he saw the heavens torn apart and the Spirit descending like a dove on him. And a voice came from heaven, "You are my Son, the Beloved; with you I am well pleased." And the Spirit immediately drove him out into the wilderness.

—Mark 1:9-12

Reflection

These days I feel like I am living in the wilderness. I'm at the same job, living and going through life in the same community, but I feel that I'm in a foreign land, a cruel, barren, dust-blown wasteland. There is deep division among people. There is anger, hatred, and a level of mistrust that I've never experienced before. It seems that our shared values of civility and respect for all people have been left behind and that we are moving ever more quickly toward irreconcilable polarization.

And yet the wilderness is a familiar, if uncomfortable, place for those of us who follow the Holy One. The people of Israel wandered for forty years in the wilderness before finding the Promised Land. Jesus was baptized and was driven into the wilderness for forty days. This Lenten season is our forty days in the wilderness. Days in which we are called to self-examination, repentance, and returning to the heart of God.

Holy Protector, I am in the wilderness, and I don't know how I will survive. Send your Spirit to blow through my life and community that I might know your presence in this place. Amen.

———

Carry This Word in Your Heart Today

Wilderness

Day 3

Giving up something for Lent is a familiar tradition for many, a variation on an old and rich tradition of self-denial known as fasting. . . . Maybe you know people who approach the season of Lent by giving up chocolate or coffee or another indulgence and then follow through with that intention until Easter. The idea of giving up something—usually a personally meaningful practice or custom—for Lent has become *one* way to fast during the season. The reasoning behind this ancient tradition focused on ways to develop openness to God. . . . This Lenten season I invite you to break from the usual custom of fasting or other form of self-denial and, instead, to fast from apathy. That means you set aside all your noncaring attitudes and move closer to the caring love of God. . . . We must move from prayer to action.

—George Hovaness Donigian, *A World Worth Saving*

Scripture

To you, O Lord, I lift up my soul.
O my God, in you I trust;
  do not let me be put to shame;
  do not let my enemies exult over me.
Do not let those who wait for you be put to shame;

let them be ashamed who are wantonly treacherous.
Make me to know your ways, O LORD;
    teach me your paths.
Lead me in your truth, and teach me,
    for you are the God of my salvation;
    for you I wait all day long.

—Psalm 25:1-5

Reflection

When I was old enough to understand that there were different seasons of the church year, my pastor-father guided me in ways I could participate in the season of Lent. The first Lenten discipline I attempted was to fast on Fridays from 12:00 p.m. to 6:00 p.m.—the day and hours, he said, that Jesus was on the cross.

In more recent years I have, like the author above, intended to fast from habits that separate me from the Holy One. I have given up worry, cynicism, or social media to help me move closer to the heart of God. I have also taken on new practices during the season of Lent. Centering Prayer and mindfulness meditation are two practices that have been helpful to my spiritual journey.

What clutters your heart or mind and gets in the way of your love of God or neighbor? What could you give up or take on during this Lenten journey?

Holy One, my mind, heart, and spirit are cluttered with attitudes and habits that separate me from you and from my neighbors. Guide me into Lenten practices that keep my heart open to Love. Amen.

CARRY THIS WORD IN YOUR HEART TODAY

Fast

Day 4

Practice saying "God is here" the next time you are assaulted by your neighbors' quarreling, see someone carelessly toss trash from a car, get drenched in an unexpected rainstorm . . . or bite into a mealy and tasteless apple. From his own experience, Saint Francis of Assisi learned that the deeper lessons of God came when one embraced all things, even that which isn't beautiful. When we turn our attention to both delightful and painful ways God can get to us through our senses, we discover yet another way to pray in the midst of our daily lives.

—Jane E. Vennard with Stephen D. Bryant,
The Way of Prayer Participant's Book

Scripture

God said to Noah and to his sons with him, "As for me, I am establishing my covenant with you and your descendants after you, and with every living creature that is with you, the birds, the domestic animals, and every animal of the earth with you, as many as came out of the ark. I establish my covenant with you, that never again shall all flesh be cut off by the waters of a flood, and never again shall there be a flood to destroy the earth." God said, "This is the sign of the covenant that I make between me and you and every living creature that is with you, for all future generations: I have set my bow in the clouds, and it shall be a sign of the covenant between me and the earth."

—Genesis 9:8-13

Reflection

It can be difficult to feel God when we are walking in the wildernesses of life. We face scary illnesses in ourselves or others, we mourn the death of a loved one, we struggle with loneliness or depression, and we wonder whether God is present with us. We witness hatred and discrimination toward ourselves, our families, our friends, and we wonder why God does not change the hardened hearts of religious and political leaders and their followers. We struggle to find a path through the conflicts going on in our churches and in our world. We see our earth groaning in travail, and we wonder whether the Creator is still watching over us.

We can, as the author suggests, practice saying, "God is here" during these times. God is here despite our feelings to the contrary. We declare God's presence as a statement of faith, an act of surrender, a path of trusting that we are not alone in whatever wilderness we find ourselves.

Holy One, you are present, even when I cannot see or feel you. Let me affirm you by saying, "God is here." Amen.

———

Carry This Word in Your Heart Today

Presence

BEING PRESENT

"Consider the lilies of the field, how they grow; they neither toil nor spin."

—Matthew 6:28

Being present may be one of the most powerful practices that we can engage in the world today. When we are in the present moment, our attention is *here*—the place where we find ourselves right now. We can listen deeply to the person with whom we are talking. We can interact fully with the community that surrounds us at work, at home, or in the world as we move through it. We are able to see through "the eyes of the present" all things—large and small—that make up our lives. If we are truly in the present moment, we are open to the movement of the Holy One. We become a channel for the Spirit's promptings in us.

When we are present, we are able to watch for the ways that multitasking takes us away from the present moment. We often find that it is not possible for us to be present with another person or with ourselves when we are also in a second or third conversation on our electronic devices. Our brains were not created to multitask. Studies have indicated that when we are doing more than one thing at a time, we are actually switching quickly between tasks rather than doing two (or more) tasks at once.

Being Present with the Holy One

Use this exercise to ground yourself in the present moment. Try the exercise several times a day this week for at least five minutes. Once you have become more familiar with the exercise, you will be able to go through the steps quickly in your mind whenever you are needing to bring yourself back to the present moment.

- Stop what you are doing and set an intention to be 100 percent present in this moment.
- Identify any potential distractions—phone, computer, television—and turn them off. Choose to be here right now.
- Close your eyes, and take several slow, deep breaths. Breathe in through your nose and out through your mouth.
- Feel your body—the parts of you touching a chair. Or feel your feet as you stand on the ground.
- Take a deep breath, in and out, and notice how your body feels. Do you detect any emotions within you? any sensations in your body?
- Take a deep breath, in and out, and notice the smells and sounds around you.
- Focus on the things that you hear. What can you hear in the present moment? Are there loud sounds? Are there soft sounds?
- Continue breathing, in and out, and feel yourself in your body. Right here. Right now.
- Now let your attention turn to the Holy One. Can you detect the presence of God? Where is God's presence? Is God beside you? Above or inside you? Turn your attention to that presence and let yourself rest in it. Keep breathing slowly and deeply, and allow yourself to rest in God's presence. Continue as long as you like.
- Now begin to bring your focus back to this present moment. As you let your senses move back into the room, remember that you can come back to this peaceful moment at any time during the day.

- Perhaps there were important words or thoughts that came to you during this time. Make note of these, and take some time later to write them down and reflect on them in a journal.
- When you are ready, open your eyes. And come back to this space.

If you have more time for this exercise, enter into a time of prayer, silently or aloud. Make a list of the things for which you are grateful. Or spend some time journaling in words or images.

Return to this grounding exercise throughout your day. Practice being present in a conversation with another person. Step outside and ground yourself in God's creation. At the end of your day, practice being in the present moment and offer in prayer the places during your day where you saw God's presence in people or situations.

Many of us have images of God that prevent us from seeing ourselves as merely resting in God's lap. But eventually words cease, requests run out, arguments stop, and we are invited simply to be with God. Not seeking a feeling. Not looking for an answer. Not actively imagining God, listening to God, or talking to God, but crawling up in the lap of Love, resting our head against Love's breast, and taking comfort in that slow, steady heartbeat of grace that says, *This is where you belong.*

—L. Roger Owens, *What We Need Is Here*

Scripture

One thing I asked of the LORD,
    that will I seek after:
to live in the house of the LORD
    all the days of my life,
to behold the beauty of the LORD,
    and to inquire in his temple.

For [God] will hide me in [God's] shelter
    in the day of trouble;
[God] will conceal me under the cover of [God's] tent;
    [God] will set me high on a rock.

Now my head is lifted up
    above my enemies all around me,
and I will offer in [God's] tent
    sacrifices with shouts of joy;
I will sing and make melody to the LORD.

Hear, O LORD, when I cry aloud,
    be gracious to me and answer me!
"Come," my heart says, "seek [God's] face!"
    Your face, LORD, do I seek.

—Psalm 27:4-8

Reflection

I love the image of resting in God's lap. This prayer exercise invites us to let go of words, feelings, and judgments, allowing ourselves to sink into the heart of God.

If sitting in God's lap is a difficult image for you, contemplate sitting safely within the protection of the Holy One. What would be the signs of that protection? Gates? Walls? Heavenly beings shielding you from harm? Or would your safe place be less concrete, more ethereal? Perhaps you see yourself surrounded by light or encircled by a healing color.

Take some time today to let yourself experience God's loving embrace. Imagine yourself hearing God say to you, "This is where you belong."

Tender God, I long to be held in your loving embrace, to feel your protection around me. Set me high upon the rock, shield me in your shelter. I am yours. Amen.

Carry This Word in Your Heart Today

Belonging

Day 6

Jesus comes to proclaim that we are God's beloved children, that what the government says we are doesn't matter, that what the powers and principalities want us to believe doesn't matter, that our brokenness doesn't matter. We are God's beloved children, and this is what matters. We are commended to live as if we know how deeply we are loved. Anxiety and worry are not our inheritance. When we find our center, our calm heart in Christ, this is the peace that cannot be taken away by the world. . . . Breath by breath we ask God's love to become our experience. Prayer by prayer we hold ourselves open to the possibility that we can live and feel and experience life as beloved children of God.

—Jane Herring, *One Day I Wrote Back*

Scripture

[God said to Abraham,] "This is my covenant with you: You shall be the ancestor of a multitude of nations. No longer shall your name be Abram, but your name shall be Abraham; for I have made you the ancestor of a multitude of nations. . . . I will establish my covenant between me and you, and your offspring after you throughout their generations, for an everlasting covenant, to be God to you and to your offspring after you. . . . As for Sarai your wife, you shall not call her Sarai, but Sarah shall be her name. I will bless her, and moreover I will give you a son by her. I will bless her, and she shall give rise to nations; kings of peoples shall come from her."

—Genesis 17:4-5, 7, 15-16

Reflection

Do you understand that you are God's beloved? Take some moments right now to hear these words from the Holy One: "You are my beloved."

Some of us know this belovedness, have known it throughout our lives. For some of us, this is an unfamiliar or even painful statement.

Pause in your quiet time today, and identify for yourself how you feel or what you think when you hear those words spoken to you. What fits and doesn't fit? What would you like to say back to God? If you cannot identify as God's beloved, what barriers get in the way? If the name is not *beloved*, what name does the Holy One give to you?

Note: If you find yourself in pain from this interior discussion, please reach out for help from a therapist, pastor, or spiritual friend. You don't have to do this alone.

Holy One, often I live in worry and anxiety. I fail to remember that I was created by you in love and that you hold me as one of your beloved creations. Whisper to me the name that you call me. I am listening. Amen.

Carry This Word in Your Heart Today

Beloved

May those without hope take heart in you, O Christ.
May those with no home find shade at your right hand.
May those near the end see beginnings;
May those at the last become first.
At the foot of your cross,
O Christ, I come in prayer.
O Christ, be my help,
O Christ, be our hope.
Amen.

—Pamela Hawkins, *Weavings*

Scripture

[God] did not despise or abhor
  the affliction of the afflicted;
[the LORD] did not hide [God's] face from me,
  but heard when I cried to [God].

From you comes my praise in the great congregation;
  my vows I will pay before those who fear [God].
The poor shall eat and be satisfied;
  those who seek him shall praise the LORD.
  May your hearts live forever!

All the ends of the earth shall remember

and turn to the LORD;
and all the families of the nations
    shall worship before [God].

—Psalm 22:24-27

Reflection

Wilderness times invite integrity, truth-telling, and lament. There is great suffering in the world, in communities, churches, and families. We can be honest in expressing to God our hopes and our fears, our anger and our despair. Our spiritual ancestors modeled for us the practice of lament, of expressing our deepest grief and sorrow to God. "Rouse yourself! Why do you sleep, O Lord?" the psalmist cries in Psalm 44:23.

And we might call out to the Holy One, "Why do the powerful punish the poor, the immigrant, the children? Where are you when Black and Brown bodies suffer from the viruses of racism and COVID-19? God of the least of these, why don't you show up when your beloveds are in danger?"

The Holy One invites us to lay our prayers at the base of Christ's cross and to know that God hears our cries. God is our hope.

Hear my cries, Almighty God, and do not abandon me! The powerful sleep in their luxurious beds and dream up new ways to oppress the weak, the displaced, the poorest among us. What shall I do, God of hope? Amen.

Carry This Word in Your Heart Today

Honesty

Grief is such a messy thing. It fills us with many ideas and images, memories and fantasies, celebration and bitter regret all at once—all superimposed upon one another. No wonder it wears us out. . . . However isolated we may feel in other areas of our lives, in our grief we are not isolated at all; we have with us not only the presence of God but the whole human race solidly with us, supporting us even when we do not allow ourselves to feel it.

—Roberta C. Bondi, *Wild Things*

Scripture

I lift up my eyes to the hills—
    from where will my help come?
My help comes from the Lord,
    who made heaven and earth.

[The Lord] will not let your foot be moved;
    [the One] who keeps you will not slumber . . .
    will neither slumber nor sleep.

The Lord is your keeper;
    the Lord is your shade at your right hand.
The sun shall not strike you by day,
    nor the moon by night.

The Lord will keep you from all evil. . . .
The Lord will keep
    your going out and your coming in
    from this time on and forevermore.

                                              —Psalm 121

Reflection

My mother passed away when I was twenty-six. Her death sent me into a dark depression. Rather than seeking help, I reached for things that would numb the grief. After a number of years of struggle, I began to make my way back to health, only to discover that the grief was still there, waiting for me to feel it.

Once I began to work on my grief, I discovered that I was not alone. I was surrounded by others who were journeying through the valley of the shadow of death. I realized that I had been held in the love of the Holy One even during the most hopeless days of my depression. I may have felt alone, but God's love was there, holding me.

These days, so many of us are weighed down with grief. May we know the love and presence of the Holy One.

Creator God, I lift my eyes to you, the source of my help. Whether I am lost in grief, loneliness, or despair, you are there, ready to comfort me. I offer to you each worry, each tear, each wound. Amen.

———

Carry This Word in Your Heart Today

Grief

Day 9

God,
Collect our tears

Tears of sadness
tears of joy

Tears of anxiety
nervous tears

Tears that don't know why they run like rivers down the face
Gracious God,
collect our tears in your bottle

And pour them back on us as life-giving water!
—Safiyah Fosua, *The Africana Worship Book: Year B*

Scripture

Jesus said, "Jerusalem, Jerusalem, the city that kills the prophets and stones those who are sent to it! How often have I desired to gather your children together as a hen gathers her brood under her wings, and you were not willing!"

—Luke 13:34

Reflection

A number of years ago, someone gave me a small, handblown glass vial made by a collective of Palestinian women. I was going through a difficult wilderness season—a season filled with tears. It was comforting to hold the little turquoise vase and imagine that God was collecting my tears.

During that season of struggle, someone told me that tears are prayers to God. I believe and have experienced that truth. Whether tears are cried in sadness, despair, anger, joy, or anxiety, they are prayers to God that need no word, no explanation.

God of sadness and joy, accept my tears as prayers to you. Receive them, hold them, and transform them to your purpose in my life. Amen.

————

Carry This Word in Your Heart Today

Tears

Day 10

Sometimes life seems unbearable. Our hearts and minds are weighed heavily upon, and we struggle to let go of all that burdens us for fear of losing the illusion of control we have over our lives. We call upon your name today, O God, that you may free us from worry and all that troubles our minds, bodies, and spirits. We put our trust in you, O God, this day and always. Amen.

—Rueben P. Job, Norman Shawchuck, and John S. Mogabgab, *A Guide to Prayer for All Who Walk with God*

Scripture

The LORD is my light and my salvation;
  whom shall I fear?
The LORD is the stronghold of my life;
  of whom shall I be afraid?

When evildoers assail me
  to devour my flesh—
my adversaries and foes—
  they shall stumble and fall.

Though an army encamp against me,
    my heart shall not fear;
though war rise up against me,
    yet I will be confident.

—Psalm 27:1-3

Reflection

Sometimes life is just too much for us. I am easily overwhelmed by the 24/7 streams of information and news that come at me. My emotions are buffeted about with each crisis, each breaking news story, each new world disaster. I am heartbroken by the changes occurring in our environment, and I feel that my own small efforts won't make much difference in a world of such vast brokenness. I feel angry and hopeless when I witness the conflicts taking place in my community of faith.

When I call my spiritual advisor to discuss the crises in my life or the world, her first question to me is often, "Did you pray?" And my answer is, usually, "No, I forgot."

How embarrassing to be a teacher of spiritual disciplines and realize that prayer is often one of the last things I think of when I'm facing a crisis. (God obviously has a sense of humor when it comes to these things.)

When I do remember to turn toward God in prayer, I find comfort and grounding. I find that God is right there waiting for me, holding me in my pain and struggle. God is my light and my stronghold.

Loving God, you are always there, even when I don't remember to reach out to you. Remind me that you are my light and salvation. Shape me with your gentle hands into the person you would have me be. Amen.

Carry This Word in Your Heart Today

Remember

Second Sunday in Lent

LAMENT

How long, O LORD? Will you forget me forever?
How long will you hide your face from me?

—Psalm 13:1

The spiritual practice of lament is central to a people walking in the wilderness. The people of Israel cried out to God during times of exile. They did not hold back on their critique of God's action or inaction. They expressed to God their thoughts and emotions, knowing that God would hear their cries.

Lament is a prayer for help that comes from a place of pain or distress. Lament gives voice to our intimate feelings, our deepest longings. Through expressing our laments, we give voice to the exiled parts of our deepest self. Lament can be part of the process of healing. We offer our concerns and our wounds to God. And, if our wounds are not healed, they are acknowledged and offered in prayer to the One who walks with us in our wilderness.

One third of the psalms are classified as psalms of lament. The psalms of lament include individual and community laments expressing both personal and communal grief and pain.

Read a Psalm of Lament

Choose a psalm of lament (see list below) and read it aloud. How does it feel to pray these words aloud to God?

Individual psalms of lament: 6, 10, 13, 22, 25, 31, 38, 44, 55, 71, 86

Corporate psalms of lament: 44, 60, 74, 79, 80, 85, 90

Write Your Own Lament

Psalms of lament follow a structure that includes at least the following elements:

- Address—Your cry to God
  "My God, my God" (Ps. 22:1).
- Complaint—Description of the problem
  "Why have you forsaken me?
     Why are you so far from helping me, from the words of my
        groaning?" (Ps. 22:1-2).
- Petition—A request for help
  "Rise up, O LORD, in your anger;
     lift yourself up against the fury of my enemies;
     awake, O my God; you have appointed a judgment" (Ps. 7:6).
- Affirmation—A statement of trust
  "But I call upon God,
     and the LORD will save me.
  Evening and morning and at noon
     I utter my complaint and moan,
     and he will hear my voice" (Ps. 55:16-17).
- Resolution—A vow of praise to God
  "O my strength, I will sing praises to you,
     for you, O God, are my fortress,
     the God who shows me steadfast love" (Ps. 59:17).

Write your own psalm of lament following the pattern above. Or pick a psalm of lament and adapt it to your situation. After you have written your psalm of lament, share it with a trusted friend or covenant group. Read it aloud to the Holy One who hears your deepest cries.

Day 11

O God, sometimes I think you have forgotten me;
sometimes my faith becomes very small.
Please remind me that you have not abandoned me,
for your faithfulness never changes.
Help me to wait with patience
and to trust that all time is in your hand.
　　—Elizabeth J. Canham, *Finding Your Voice in the Psalms*

Scripture

From the wilderness of Sin the whole congregation of the Israelites journeyed by stages, as the LORD commanded. They camped at Rephidim, but there was no water for the people to drink. The people quarreled with Moses, and said, "Give us water to drink." Moses said to them, "Why do you quarrel with me? Why do you test the LORD?" But the people thirsted there for water; and the people complained against Moses and said, "Why did you bring us out of Egypt, to kill us and our children and livestock with thirst?" So Moses cried out to the LORD, "What shall I do with this people? They are almost ready to stone me." The LORD said to Moses, "Go on ahead of the people, and take some of the elders of Israel with you; take in your hand the staff with which you struck the Nile, and go. I will be standing there in front of you on the rock at Horeb. Strike the rock, and water will come out of it, so that the people may drink." Moses did so, in the sight of the elders of Israel. He called the place Massah and Meribah, because the Israelites quarreled and tested the LORD, saying, "Is the LORD among us or not?"

—Exodus 17:1-7

Reflection

Sometimes I wonder, *Where are you today, God? Do you not see what is going on here in this world? People are suffering! The earth is groaning in pain! Are you there? Are you listening?*

We see in the scriptures that these wonderings are not new. Our spiritual ancestors, the Israelite people, demanded of God, "Why did you bring us out of Egypt, to kill us . . . with thirst?" (Exod. 17:3).

Whether our deserts are personal or corporate, lament can be the prayer language to help us on our journey through the wilderness.

Holy One, creator of all things, where are you today? Do you not care about the poor and vulnerable? Will you not help us save this planet that is our home? Hear me! Help us, I pray. Amen.

———————

Carry This Word in Your Heart Today

Lament

Day 12

God is with us behind our defensive walls, our locked doors. The doors are not kicked in, nor are the walls and masks torn away. God understands that our walls and masks grew from our pain and fear, from traumas that affected our ability to trust. In time the doors themselves will be healed, and our masks will become living flesh again when we realize we no longer need them for our survival. But in the meantime, the healing love shines in our defended darkness, and God's Holy Spirit is breathed upon us.

—Flora Slosson Wuellner, *Miracle*

Scripture

Ho, everyone who thirsts,
    come to the waters;
and you that have no money,
    come, buy and eat!
Come, buy wine and milk
    without money and without price.
Why do you spend your money for that which is not bread,
    and your labor for that which does not satisfy?
Listen carefully to me, and eat what is good,
    and delight yourselves in rich food.
Incline your ear, and come to me;

listen, so that you may live.
I will make with you an everlasting covenant,
    my steadfast, sure love for David.

—Isaiah 55:1-3

Reflection

God created in each of us a yearning for healing and wholeness. No matter how deep or devastating our wounds, we have within us a profound desire and ability to mend, to thrive. God provides for us what we need to heal.

In my years of recovery from trauma, I was fortunate to have a community around me that helped me navigate the wilderness of depression. When I did not think I could make it, I reached out to the members of my support team for their assistance. When I felt alone, they sat with me. When I did not know what step to take next, they walked beside me. When I cried tears of sorrow and betrayal, they comforted me. When I could not believe in the Holy One, they believed on my behalf.

God of healing, you sit with the wounded and bind up their hurts. Send your healing love into all the places of despair in this vast world. Amen.

Carry This Word in Your Heart Today

Healing

Day 13

Hope is not immune to attack. Hope is subject to attack by fear, worry, and doubt. Yes, in times of difficulty, we may begin to question whether God's promises will actually come to pass. In times of great challenge, we may begin to wonder whether or not we will actually make it out of hard situations to experience true victory in our lives over the forces of evil within our world. Holding on to hope can be particularly challenging when what we have hoped for appears to be the furthest thing from actually happening in our time.

Yet in the face of these attacks, hope proves essential to life's journey. It is the very essence of hope that gives us the strength to endure seasons of great challenge and difficulty. Hope must never lose its voice!

—Michael W. Waters, *Freestyle*

Scripture

Since we are justified by faith, we have peace with God through our Lord Jesus Christ, through whom we have obtained access to this grace in which we stand; and we boast in our hope of sharing the glory of God. And not only that, but we also boast in our sufferings, knowing that suffering produces endurance, and endurance produces character, and character produces hope, and hope does not disappoint us, because

God's love has been poured into our hearts through the Holy Spirit that
has been given to us.

—Romans 5:1-5

Reflection

It is easy to lose hope during seasons of wilderness. Our hope crum-
bles under the weight of overwhelming evil and injustice in our world.
Watching the news, some days, sends us into cynicism, fatalism, or
hopelessness. We despair as we face illnesses, aging, and death. We
worry about mass shootings and hatred of "the other."

The people of Israel modeled for us a way that leads to hope. They
grumbled and complained in the wilderness, but the Holy One gave
them what they needed to survive. The psalmists cry out in despair and,
in the next breath, praise God's faithfulness. (See Psalm 22.) God continues to promise, "I know the plans I have for you . . . plans for your
welfare and not for harm, to give you a future with hope" (Jer. 29:11).

God invites us to turn toward hope even on our bleakest days. God
calls us to trust in God and God's promises, to become voices of hope
in the world.

*God, I'm losing hope these days. Sit with me in my hopelessness and despair.
Stay by me even when I grumble and whine. Show me glimpses of hope that
I might declare your loving presence. Amen.*

Carry This Word in Your Heart Today

Hope

The tree of our soul requires two basic initial ingredients that are essential for its future: good soil and strong roots. However, we cannot grow strong roots without soil. . . . What is good soil for the soul? With what do we fill this hole we've created? Generally good soil is made up of about 25 percent water and 25 percent air (made mostly of oxygen and nitrogen). The other half is made of stone, clay, and organic matter—decaying plant and animal life. We are not surprised to learn that soil is half air and water—things we know we need in order to live as much as trees do. But what is the spiritual equivalent of good dirt? Answer: *humility.* Just as trees wither and die without good soil, our soul will not grow without humility. With that soil in place, roots can form in the earth, and as they grow deep and strong, the tree moves out of the ground and toward the light.

—Christopher Maricle, *Deeply Rooted*

Scripture

[Jesus] told this parable: "A man had a fig tree planted in his vineyard; and he came looking for fruit on it and found none. So he said to the gardener, 'See here! For three years I have come looking for fruit on this fig tree, and still I find none. Cut it down! Why should it be wasting the soil?' He replied, 'Sir, let it alone for one more year, until I dig around it and put manure on it. If it bears fruit next year, well and good; but if not, you can cut it down.'"

—Luke 13:6-9

Reflection

In these days of wilderness, I find myself yearning for groundedness. There was a period of months, recently, when I was drawing trees, including their underground root systems. My journal was filled with reflections on "taking root," "getting grounded," "finding my foundation."

I'm struck with the images of humility in today's quote. What role does humility play in surviving our wilderness journeys? The word *humility* is derived from the Latin *humilitas*, meaning "grounded" or "from the earth."

What does it take to be grounded? It requires the good soil of balance, of self-care, of nurturing body, mind, and spirit. It requires stability, staying put in one place long enough to let roots sink down into rich soil. It requires caring not only for self but also for other people and for the environment in which we live. All these are elements of being grounded in humility.

God of life, I want to be grounded in you. May I grow my roots deep into your love, hope, and strength. Infuse me with humility that I might remember that you are the source of all life. Amen.

Carry This Word in Your Heart Today

Humility

Day 15

Anxiety fills my life.
Busyness is the order of the day.
Crowded schedules, shopping sprees and misplaced priorities
    mask my deepest pain.
My heart is crying out for true intimacy.
Lord, draw near to me and let me sit at your feet.
      —Junius Dotson, *The Africana Worship Book: Year C*

Scripture

God spoke all these words: I am the LORD your God, who brought you out of the land of Egypt, out of the house of slavery; you shall have no other gods before me. You shall not make for yourself an idol, whether in the form of anything that is in heaven above, or that is on the earth beneath, or that is in the water under the earth. You shall not bow down to them or worship them.

      —Exodus 20:1-5

Reflection

What are the other gods before which I bow? These are not difficult to identify. The number one culprit (idol) is my mobile phone. I'm addicted to the presence of it. If I have misplaced my phone or intentionally leave it in the office when I go to a meeting, I feel anxious, vulnerable, like something is missing.

The more insecure I feel about the state of the world, the more susceptible I am to putting other gods before the Holy One. I fill my heart with empty things, with busyness, with entertainment. I worship the idols of retirement savings, career advancement, or consumerism.

The Holy One invites us to true intimacy, to a relationship that feeds us with abundant love and grace rather than empty worship of the things of the world.

Loving God, let me put down all the idols, the addictions, the obsessions that keep me from you. Draw me near and let me sit at your feet. Amen.

Carry This Word in Your Heart Today

Intimacy

It is not you who shape God,
  it is God who shapes you.
If, then, you are the work of God,
  await the hand of the artist who does all things in due
  season.
Offer the Potter your heart,
  soft and tractable,
  and keep the form in which the Artist has fashioned you.
Let your clay be moist,
  lest you grow hard and lose the imprint of the Potter's
  fingers.
  —Irenaeus (2nd century), *The Upper Room Worshipbook*

Scripture

O God, you are my God, I seek you,
  my soul thirsts for you;
my flesh faints for you,
  as in a dry and weary land where there is no water.
So I have looked upon you in the sanctuary,
  beholding your power and glory.
Because your steadfast love is better than life,
  my lips will praise you.
So I will bless you as long as I live;
  I will lift up my hands and call on your name.

My soul is satisfied as with a rich feast,
  and my mouth praises you with joyful lips
when I think of you on my bed,
  and meditate on you in the watches of the night;
for you have been my help,
  and in the shadow of your wings I sing for joy.
My soul clings to you;
  your right hand upholds me.

—Psalm 63:1-8

Reflection

My spirit hungers and thirsts for God. My heart desires to be shaped by
the Holy One, to be clay in the hands of the potter. I imagine myself as
soft, red clay in the strong hands of the Creator of the Universe. I feel
the deep dryness within me quenched by God's abundant living water.
My soul cries out with joy that I am beloved of God.

These are gifts of the present moment, of slowing down enough to
listen to what I am yearning for. These are gifts of the Holy One who
loves and cares for me even I have wandered away.

*Holy One, my body, soul, and spirit hunger and thirst for you. Here in this
barren wilderness, fill me with your living water. Shape me into the one you
would have me become. Amen.*

Carry This Word in Your Heart Today

Hunger

Third Sunday in Lent

LECTIO DIVINA

"The word is near you,
  on your lips and in your heart."

—Romans 10:8

Lectio divina, from the Latin "divine reading," is an ancient practice of praying the scriptures. *Lectio divina* invites the reader to interact with the text using the eyes and ears of the heart by asking the question, "What is the Holy One saying to me in this passage?" The practice traditionally consists of four steps: reading (*lectio*), reflecting on (*meditatio*), responding to (*oratio*), and resting in (*contemplatio*). In *lectio divina,* the scripture is read for formation rather than information. The underlying question is this: "What is God saying to me in this moment?"

Origen, in the third century, believed that Christians could meet God in scripture. In a letter to Saint Gregory, Origen wrote, "When you devote yourself to the divine reading . . . seek the meaning of divine words which is hidden from most people."[1]

The four steps of *lectio divina* are most commonly used with scripture. However, this process can be used any number of ways to help the "reader" listen more deeply to God.

Using *Lectio Divina*

In the process of *lectio divina*, the scripture passage is read four times, each time, moving more deeply into the text, listening to the ways God is present. Before you begin, pick out a passage of scripture to pray. *Lectio divina* works best with a shorter passage of no more than several verses.

1. Reading (*lectio*)
   Read through the passage slowly. Listen for the word or phrase that jumps out at you, that catches your attention. What word or phrase calls to you or sticks in your memory? As you hear the word, gently take it into your heart and silently recite or ponder the word.

2. Reflecting On (*meditatio*)
   The second time you read through the text, meditate on the word or phrase that speaks to you. Let it interact with your thoughts, your hopes, your memories. Consider how the word or phrase is touching your life today.

3. Responding To (*oratio*)
   As you read the text a third time, consider how God is calling you forth into doing or being through this scripture. Allow God to use these words to touch you and shape you in your life today.

4. Resting In (*contemplatio*)
   After the final reading, let the text rest in you. Spend about ten minutes in silent contemplation. Let your mind and heart be open to the movement of the Spirit in you.

Using *Lectio Divina* with Other "Texts"

Lectio divina is a bit like the "Swiss Army Knife" of spiritual tools. The process can be used with many different types of "texts" on our spiritual journey. In addition to scripture, we can use the process of reading, reflecting, responding, and resting to hear God's guidance through images, news articles, injustices, and life events. Instead of sliding into worry, resentment, or fear about something that happened to us, we can follow the four steps of *lectio divina* and listen for God's response. In *lectio divina*, we take a step back from the story or situation, ask ourselves what caught our attention, hold that thing in our hearts, and invite the Holy One to speak to us through it. Using the steps of *lectio divina* helps us to pray about an event rather than merely worry that it happened. Through *lectio divina*, we ask, "God, what are you calling me to do or be through this?"

Follow the four steps above ("Using *Lectio Divina*") to find God's calling through images, news articles, injustices, and life events:

- An image. Look deeply at a photograph or piece of art and see what your eyes are drawn to. What catches your attention or sticks in your memory?
- A story in the news. As you read or hear the article, what words, details, or images catch your attention and stick in your memory?
- Injustice. As you read, hear about, see, or remember this experience, what word, image, or feeling catches your attention, jumps out at you, sticks in your memory?
- An event from your life. As you remember what happened to you, what image or feeling catches your attention, jumps out at you, sticks in your memory?

Regardless of the text we use, *lectio divina* helps open our minds, hearts, and spirits to the movement of the Holy One in our lives.

Day 17

You and I share at least one task in common: prayer. Jesus Christ calls us to pray. Our prayers cast out fear and open us to hospitality and friendship. Our prayers give us wisdom and courage to initiate relationships, to extend grace to strangers, and to entertain angels unaware. Our daily labor in prayer encourages us to fast from apathy, to serve others, feed the hungry, challenge injustice, and be the body of Christ in the world.

—George Hovaness Donigian, *A World Worth Saving*

Scripture

Let all who are faithful
    offer prayer to you;
at a time of distress, the rush of mighty waters
    shall not reach them.
You are a hiding place for me;
    you preserve me from trouble;
    you surround me with glad cries of deliverance.

I will instruct you and teach you the way you should go;
    I will counsel you with my eye upon you. . . .

Be glad in the LORD and rejoice, O righteous,
    and shout for joy, all you upright in heart.

—Psalm 32:6-8, 11

Reflection

The author of today's quote is not describing a "just Jesus and me" sort of prayer. This shared labor of prayer to which we are called is rooted in and bears fruit in action. In these days of exile, the vulnerable earth is exploited. Borders of countries around the world are being closed to people who look, speak, or worship differently. Hate crimes are on the rise. In all of this, we are called to prayer coupled with action.

When I connect my wholehearted prayer life with action, I move beyond the paralysis of despair into an action-oriented outlet for my prayers. We are called to embody Christ, to be Christ's hands, feet, and heart in a broken world. May we consider how we are called into action through our prayers.

Holy One, show me how to act through my prayers and pray through my actions. Amen.

————————

Carry This Word in Your Heart Today

Prayer

Dear God, help us to see that we are much more than our scars. You have made us far too complex to be defined by what is without as opposed to what is within. Forgive us for the times we have devalued ourselves, as well as for the times we have devalued others, for as the psalmist wrote in lyric, "I praise you, for I am fearfully and wonderfully made. Wonderful are your works; that I know very well" (Ps. 139:14). In Jesus' name. Amen.

—Michael W. Waters, *Freestyle*

Scripture

From now on, therefore, we regard no one from a human point of view; even though we once knew Christ from a human point of view, we know him no longer in that way. So if anyone is in Christ, there is a new creation: everything old has passed away; see, everything has become new! All this is from God, who reconciled us to himself through Christ, and has given us the ministry of reconciliation.

—2 Corinthians 5:16-18

Reflection

We all carry scars and the wounds that created them. Some scars are more visible than others, but it's common for wounds to get reinjured in the stresses of daily living. Richard Rohr writes, "The place of the wound is the place of the greatest gift."[1]

This has been true for me. I have become the person I am today because of my wounds and their healing by the Holy One. I believe that my creativity, my capacity for empathy, and my resilience are gifts from my wounding and healing. I now am able to offer these gifts back to the world. I am grateful for the grace that others have given me as I have moved through the healing of my wounds toward becoming "a new creation." May I offer that same grace to others.

Holy One, healer and transformer of wounds, fill me with grace for myself and others during the times when my wounds are tender. Amen.

Carry This Word in Your Heart Today

Grace

My spiritual director used to say to me, "Trevor, sometimes God stands at the door of the room of your life and places a hand on the light switch and dims it a bit. Then in the darkness God whispers, 'Will you learn to trust me in the dark? Will you love me even when you don't feel my presence?'" In these moments of darkness, I have found a certain practice very helpful. I have what I call a *love-word* for God that I carry in my heart and repeat when I am in the dark. Often when God feels far away, I say this word to God with all the faith and hope and love in my heart. It has the effect of keeping me consciously connected to God's loving presence even when I do not feel it.

—Trevor Hudson, *Invitations of Jesus*

Scripture

Once you were darkness, but now in the Lord you are light. Live as children of light—for the fruit of the light is found in all that is good and right and true.

—Ephesians 5:8-9

Reflection

My first book was called *Child of the Light*. I wrote the book not long after I had come out of a season of darkness triggered by work on traumatic experiences I had as a child. I remember the day when I suddenly realized that I was seeing colors again. I hadn't realized that during my depression, the light had dimmed. But then, the world was once again awash with color instead of gray.

During the years I walked in the darkness of the wilderness, I was not journeying alone. I was surrounded by helpers and healers, friends and church members who traveled with me. In the moments when I could not feel the presence of the Holy One, I trusted the presence of those who were walking with me. These people were trusting and believing in God on my behalf. This host of friends and professionals were God's instruments of healing who loved me back into being. And I'm very grateful.

God of love, may I be the presence of love for someone who is struggling. Let me be light for the world and light for others. Amen.

Carry This Word in Your Heart Today

Light

Day 20

Faithfulness is consecration in overalls. It is the steady acceptance and performance of the common duty and immediate task without any reference to personal preferences—because it is there to be done and so is a manifestation of the Will of God. . . . Faithfulness means continuing quietly with the job we have been given, in the situation where we have been placed; not yielding to the restless desire for change. It means tending the lamp quietly for God without wondering how much longer it has got to go on.

—Evelyn Underhill, *Writings of Evelyn Underhill*

Scripture

The LORD is my shepherd, I shall not want.
    [The LORD] makes me lie down in green pastures;
[The LORD] leads me beside still waters;
    [The LORD] restores my soul.
[The LORD] leads me in right paths
    for his name's sake.

Even though I walk through the darkest valley,
    I fear no evil;
for you are with me;
    your rod and your staff—
    they comfort me.

You prepare a table before me
    in the presence of my enemies;
you anoint my head with oil;
    my cup overflows.
Surely goodness and mercy shall follow me
    all the days of my life,
and I shall dwell in the house of the LORD
    my whole life long.

—Psalm 23

Reflection

Some of our journeys take us through "the darkest valley." But most of our life's tasks are mundane: discerning the next right thing to do, living our best in the situations we encounter. This is faithful living, "consecration in overalls," as Evelyn Underhill names it.

Whether we are walking through valleys or through ordinary days, the practices that keep us rooted are the same. When things are going well, we sometimes lose focus and cut back on the habits that keep us grounded. Faithfulness helps us stay on the path, keeping us connected with the Holy One, so that we are ready to face whatever valleys we encounter.

When we live in faithfulness, we are conscious of our callings in the small things—being kind to all, sharing light and love rather than gloom and cynicism, thinking of others more than we think of ourselves, listening for the Spirit's urging in our relationships with others.

Holy One, may I be as faithful in the small things as I am during crises. Amen.

Carry This Word in Your Heart Today

Faithfulness

Day 21

We are part of a larger reality, a vast, vibrant community of meadow and mountain, water and sky, a great rush of life rich with possibility but also bounded by necessity. All things come and go. Whether this be a formula for weary resignation or for tranquil acceptance of the inevitable, the most we can hope for is that all things come and all things go over and over again.

—John S. Mogabgab, *Weavings*

Scripture

O give thanks to the LORD, for [the LORD] is good;
    for [God's] steadfast love endures forever.
Let the redeemed of the LORD say so,
    those [God] redeemed from trouble
and gathered in from the lands,
    from the east and from the west,
    from the north and from the south. . . .

Let them thank the LORD for . . . steadfast love,
    for [God's] wonderful works to humankind.

—Psalm 107:1-3, 8

Reflection

Why is death such a surprise? We know it is coming for all of us, but when it happens, it's shocking. "How could this be?" we cry. "They were just here, and now they are gone." Perhaps our shock is due to a false sense that we can somehow control the things that are going on around us. Perhaps it's just denial that death is a part of life.

John S. Mogabgab said it so well: "All things come and all things go over and over again." God created a circle of life in this universe in which we live. We are born, the next descendants of our ancestors who have been here since the beginning of time. Our cells are made up of ancient particles. We are knit together with all of creation, one small element of God's enduring, steadfast love that includes birds and mammals, seas and mountains, stars and planets. Our presence is a gift, and then, like all things, we die and become a part of everlasting Love.

Let us live each day in joy, knowing that every moment is a gift from the Holy One, knowing that we are God's beloved.

Loving God, let me live each moment knowing that it is a gift from you. I offer gratitude for the enduring, steadfast love that holds us all. Amen.

―――――――

Carry This Word in Your Heart Today

Acceptance

Day 22

Hope is the lifeline tossed out to us from God. It sustains us when we feel like we are drowning, and God gently pulls us and the lifeline toward the shores of spiritual growth. With hope, we also have faith—not faith that we will be spared pain and despair but faith in the God who will lead us through the difficult times.

—John R. Wimmer, *Blessed Endurance*

Scripture

By grace you have been saved through faith, and this is not your own doing; it is the gift of God—not the result of works, so that no one may boast. For we are what [God] has made us, created in Christ Jesus for good works, which God prepared beforehand to be our way of life.

—Ephesians 2:8-10

Reflection

The news is bleak these days, and I find that I need to limit my intake of news from any source. I am easily overwhelmed and have a tendency to spin out into hopelessness and despair. I wonder where God is in all this mess—a world crisis of COVID-19, climate change, mass shootings, and escalations of overt racism and xenophobia.

Wimmer says that "hope is the lifeline tossed out to us by God." It sustains us when we feel that we are about to drown. I see hope when I look for God's presence in friends, family members, and coworkers. I find God's lifeline when I pay attention to the seasons of the year as they turn from winter to spring, summer to fall. I feel hope when I gather with my community for a service of worship and hear voices raised in song or prayer.

God of hope, throw me your lifeline. I am in danger of drowning in despair and hopelessness. Support my tender faith in your desire for good in the world. Amen.

Carry This Word in Your Heart Today

Trust

TRUST

Surely God is my salvation;
    I will trust, and will not be afraid,
for the LORD GOD is my strength and my might;
    [the LORD GOD] has become my salvation.
                     —Isaiah 12:2

How do we trust in the midst of uncertainty? In the midst of injustice and a world filled with hatred? In the midst of financial insecurity or illness? How do we trust when all around us seems to be falling apart? When it seems that God is not present or worthy of our trust?

We trust even when there seems to be no reason to trust. The dictionary defines *trust* this way: "*Verb*. To commit or place in one's care or keeping." As followers of Christ, we commit our care and keeping to the Holy One, the Creator of all things. And *trust* becomes a spiritual practice.

Daniel Wolpert, a healer, student of the spiritual life, and writer says, "A prayer practice is just that: practice. It is taking time to learn how to listen for God. It is taking time to see the hand of God at work in our lives."[1]

Trust is the solution to fear and uncertainty. We, like the psalmists, put our trust in God.

How to Do a Trust Inventory

Take some time today to do a trust inventory. Draw a grid with three columns. Then work through the answers to the following questions.

1. In the first column, list of your fears. Let there be no judgment. Write down the fears, no matter how rational or irrational, no matter how big or how small.

2. In the second column put your answers this question: How are my fears getting in the way of my full participation in life? How are they getting in the way of my love of God, of neighbor, or of myself?

3. In the third column, offer each fear to God. Write your own prayer or adapt this one: "Creator of the Universe, I offer [specific fear] to you. You know it already, and you love me just the same. Take away my fear that I might trust in you."

4. Finally, turn toward trust. Below the grid, write an affirmation of your trust in the Holy One. Write your own prayer or adapt this one: "God of life, you know my fears, and you accept them as an offering from me. You are the one who made me. You knit me together in my mother's womb. I trust in you, for you are my hope and my salvation."

Spend some time in prayer and reflection. Journal about what you learned doing this inventory. Write a list of the things for which you are grateful.

The tender love that our good Lord has for all who will be saved . . . comforts quickly and sweetly, explaining in this way: . . . "All will be well, and every kind of thing will be well." These words were shown quite tenderly, with no hint of blame toward me or any who would be safe.

—Julian of Norwich, *Writings of Julian of Norwich*

Scripture

This is the covenant that I will make with the house of Israel after those days, says the LORD: I will put my law within them, and I will write it on their hearts; and I will be their God, and they shall be my people.

—Jeremiah 31:33

Reflection

Julian of Norwich, who lived in England in the 1300s at the time of The Black Death, wrote words of hope that still speak to us today in times of crisis and pandemic. Julian is the saint of my heart. Her message that "all will be well" is the one that I most often need to hear. From my worry and gloomiest places, I ask, "Will everything be OK?" It is as though Julian wrote for all of us who ask that question in anxiety or despair.

This God of love that Julian knew is the very God who offered a covenant to the people of Israel. This God has tenderly written on our hearts to show that we belong to God. And we, in turn, are written on the heart of God, molded by the tender hands of the Creator. God has claimed us as God's people. And all will be well.

Holy One, you have written your Love on my heart, and I am held in yours. Remind me over and over again that "all will be well." Amen.

———

Carry This Word in Your Heart Today

Tenderness

When we experience anxiety, most of us simply want to make it go away. It is an unpleasant feeling. . . . Often our unfinished business from long ago surfaces when anxiety enters the systems in which we live, work, and worship. In spiritual direction or therapy we may discover that a good deal of our anxiety during systems change is more about our family of origin than about the situation at hand. . . . Yet the source of the problem is not anxiety. Therapists encourage anxious clients to "sit" with their anxiety so as to make decisions out of freedom rather than fear. . . . Our conviction that we are deeply loved and that God will not abandon us provides a path for us to move through anxiety. We acknowledge God's presence with us at an emotional level while in the anxiety-producing event. The capacity to *respond* instead of *react* to anxiety-provoking events has much to do with our general sense of security.

—Elaine A. Heath, *God Unbound*

Scripture

Thus says the LORD,
    who makes a way in the sea,
    a path in the mighty waters,
who brings out chariot and horse,

army and warrior;
they lie down, they cannot rise,
    they are extinguished, quenched like a wick:
Do not remember the former things,
    or consider the things of old.
I am about to do a new thing;
    now it springs forth, do you not perceive it?
I will make a way in the wilderness
    and rivers in the desert.
The wild animals will honor me,
    the jackals and the ostriches;
for I give water in the wilderness,
    rivers in the desert,
to give drink to my chosen people,
    the people whom I formed for myself
so that they might declare my praise.

—Isaiah 43:16-21

Anxiety permeates the world in which we live. When I am living in anxiety, I am not in the present moment. I am triggered by old fears and unhealed wounds.

Our siblings of color live with the anxiety created by generations of systemic racism. Indigenous peoples occupying this country were victims of genocide at the hands of Europeans. Those whose ancestors came to this country as enslaved Africans have lived through generations of trauma—chattel slavery being replaced by the slavery of poverty and institutional racism. In this "country of freedom," we have passed "whites only" immigration policies. We have enforced our own apartheid through laws and policies, imprisoning Japanese Americans in internment camps, closing our borders to those seeking asylum, separating family members from one another, and locking children in cages at the border.

The words of George Floyd, "I can't breathe," have become a symbol of a movement of protest and liberation. A remembering of the choking weight of generational trauma, of white supremacy kneeling on the necks of Black and Brown bodies. May the Holy One do a new thing in this world through the marching, the singing, the declaration that #BlackLivesMatter. May God use us to create "a [new] way in the wilderness and the rivers of the desert" (Isa. 43:19). May we follow this new way, offering life and hope and breath for all people struggling through the desert.

Loving God, today, let me breathe on behalf of those who are afraid, those who carry generations of trauma and anxiety. Let each breath call out for the new thing that is coming. May it be so. Amen.

Carry This Word in Your Heart Today

Breathe

Reconciliation is not a hasty process, proclaiming peace where there is no peace, ignoring injustice and human suffering. Reconciliation is intimately connected with justice, with right relations. As Christians, we must restore the work of reconciliation from the periphery to the center of the life and witness of the church where it belongs. My dream is that every church becomes a neighborhood reconciliation center.

—Thomas Porter, *The Spirit and Art of Conflict Transformation*

Scripture

"Very truly, I tell you, unless a grain of wheat falls into the earth and dies, it remains just a single grain; but if it dies, it bears much fruit. Those who love their life lose it, and those who hate their life in this world will keep it for eternal life. Whoever serves me must follow me, and where I am, there will my servant be also. Whoever serves me, the Father will honor."

—John 12:24-26

Reflection

The Holy One transforms people and systems and calls us to a ministry of reconciliation. (See 2 Corinthians 5:11-20.) In this fractured wilderness season, I am more likely to retreat into myself than to reach out to others across differences. I am overwhelmed by what I see happening in our communities, churches, nations, and world and would rather escape into the bubble of my social media accounts where everyone seems to agree with me.

What would it be like to stop regarding others through human eyes? To, instead, see each person as beloved of God, someone that we are called to love as we love ourselves? I must confess that I find it difficult to imagine myself sitting down with an enemy and knowing deeply that we are both beloved of God.

But Christ calls us to love rather than hate, to open hardened hearts to the fears and pain of other human beings, despite their personal belief system or political view.

Holy One, you call me to a ministry of reconciliation that seems too difficult to achieve. Give me eyes to see the belovedness in the other. Soften and open my heart to those I know as "other." Amen.

Carry This Word in Your Heart Today

Reconciliation

An altar, a pew, a seat on the bus, a kitchen table: all become holy places when we confess before God. Today, in this holy place, God meets us, hears us and forgives us. In this holy place, God empowers us with genuine love to share with a hurting world. Be for God, a holy loving people.
—Kwasi I. Kena, *The Africana Worship Book: Year A*

Scripture

Create in me a clean heart, O God,
    and put a new and right spirit within me.
Do not cast me away from your presence,
    and do not take your holy spirit from me.
Restore to me the joy of your salvation,
    and sustain in me a willing spirit.

—Psalm 51:10-12

Reflection

I spent a week working on this book at one of my holy places: a family cabin in the Colorado mountains. I love being in that space, remembering vacations with parents and grandparents, walking the road by the river, sitting in the kitchen where so many pancakes have been cooked and eaten. The cabin is a sacred place for me. But we find holy spaces everywhere if we keep our hearts open to the movement of God's Spirit.

The grocery store parking lot became a holy space when I pulled a banana out of my grocery bag for a man who was hungry. I found the Holy One over soup at Panera as I listened to the heart of my friend who is living with HIV. The airport baggage claim area became a holy place when a fellow traveler asked me about the book on spirituality I had been reading on the plane.

Watch for the presence of the Holy One.

Holy One, give me eyes to see your presence in each moment. May I find you in the most unexpected places. Amen.

Carry This Word in Your Heart Today

Watch

Day 27

During the Lenten season I begin sprouting seeds which will later green the gardens of the tiny farm I live on. I farm that I may set my hands into the body of the earth. And, yes, the body of creation groans (Romans 8:22) when the body of humanity lives as if unembodied and separated from the earth, as if incarnation does not grant holiness and healing. Typically, the degradation of the environment goes hand in hand with the degradation of different members of the human body. Sallie McFague encourages us to view all of creation as God's Body. This metaphor, she argues, allows us to give attention that invites the discovery of beauty and suffering, which calls forth our love and compassion. However, again if we do not treasure the embodied relationship within our own existence, if we are not compassionate and connected with our own bodies, we will be hard-pressed to see and touch the body of the earth with caring eyes, heart, and hand.

—Regina M. Laroche, *Weavings*

Scripture

When the LORD restored the fortunes of Zion,
>   we were like those who dream.
Then our mouth was filled with laughter,

and our tongue with shouts of joy;
then it was said among the nations,
    "The LORD has done great things for them."
The LORD has done great things for us,
    and we rejoiced.

Restore our fortunes, O LORD,
    like the watercourses in the Negeb.
May those who sow in tears
    reap with shouts of joy.
Those who go out weeping,
    bearing the seed for sowing,
shall come home with shouts of joy,
    carrying their sheaves.

—Psalm 126:1-6

Reflection

I grew up watching my maternal grandfather work his backyard garden. (When I say "backyard garden" I don't mean a garden *within* the backyard. The garden *was* the backyard.) Grandpa had a deeply spiritual relationship with the earth. Grandpa taught me that he was not the gardener; he was only the steward who planted the seeds. "It's God's garden," Grandpa would tell me. "God's the one who sends the sun and the rain and makes the seeds to grow." His humility invited me to see myself as a steward of God's creation.

These days, most of us don't grow our own food. We buy our fruits and vegetables from the store, co-op, or farmer's market. We are consumers of the labor of farmers all over the world. Yet, we each have a role in creation. We can offer gratitude for those who grew the food, advocate for justice for those who harvest the crops, and fight for a living wage for people who transport, unpack, display, and cook the food we consume.

We can care for God's creation through our responsible use of the earth's resources. Each time we conserve water or fuel, make a choice to

recycle, or consider the ways our choices impact the earth, we participate in the care of God's creation.

Bless this creation of yours, loving God. Let me walk gently on the earth
as your steward, as one who seeks justice for and protection of all creation.
Amen.

Carry This Word in Your Heart Today

Creation

Day 28

I'm learning the importance of rest. If always on the go, I'm exhausted. I need some quiet time. My physical health depends upon it. My emotional health depends on slowing down. To deal with the stress of life, I need a time of calm. My spiritual life depends on it. I can't make it on my own but depend on my faithful Savior, Jesus Christ.

—J. David Muyskens, *Sacred Breath*

Scripture

Out of the depths I cry to you, O LORD.
   Lord, hear my voice!
Let your ears be attentive
   to the voice of my supplications!

If you, O LORD, should mark iniquities,
   Lord, who could stand?
But there is forgiveness with you,
   so that you may be revered.

I wait for the LORD, my soul waits,
   and in [God's] word I hope;
my soul waits for the Lord
   more than those who watch for the morning,
   more than those who watch for the morning.

—Psalm 130:1-6

Reflection

These days, I find it hard to rest. I am diligent in my self-care: sleep, exercise, prayer and meditation, time with my spiritual director and therapist. All these things are part of the delicate balance that helps me stay healthy and whole in my life. But I'm realizing, I never stop *doing*. Sleep has become another task to check off of my self-care to-do list.

I am wondering whether my drivenness has become one more way to mask the discomfort I feel at finding myself in this space of exile, of wilderness. I keep busy so I don't have to feel the fear and anxiety that fills my heart.

When I get in touch with myself, I realize that my body and spirit thirst for rest, for spaciousness, for quiet and solitude.

Loving God, my soul thirsts for you more than those who watch for the morning. Amen.

————————

Carry This Word in Your Heart Today

Rest

Fifth Sunday in Lent

COMPASSION

The LORD is good to all,
and [God's] compassion is over all that [has been] made.
—Psalm 145:9

The root of the word *compassion—compati*—literally means "to bear, suffer." In Hebrew, the word translated as *compassion* comes from the root word *rehem,* meaning "womb." When we have compassion for another, we have the sort of love that a parent has for a child.

In this season of exile, there is so much hurt in the world. It is easy to become overwhelmed and incapacitated by the level of pain and need of our fellow human beings and the world in which we live. How do we find the healthy balance of caring that lies somewhere between compassion and numbing as we witness so much crisis and turmoil?

I wonder sometimes whether Jesus ever felt "compassion fatigue," whether he ever felt so overwhelmed that he couldn't open his heart to anything more. Scripture tells us about how Jesus dealt with all the needs around him. First, he took action. He touched people, listened to them, and healed them. He gave of himself whenever he could. Second, he prayed. He lived his life in touch with the Creator. He sought God and made time for God. Third, he took time apart. He went away in a boat. He went up a hill and left his disciples behind. He sought out times to be alone with God.

A Blessing Exercise

The Buddhist tradition has passed down to us an ancient practice called loving-kindness meditation. It is "a practice of cultivating understanding, love, and compassion by looking deeply, first for ourselves and then for others."[1] Know that as we pray this prayer, we join in with many others around the world who are also praying with and on behalf of those who are suffering. The following is an exercise based on loving-kindness meditation.[2]

Begin by finding a comfortable and quiet place to pray the blessing prayer. Take several slow, deep breaths while letting go of any tension in your neck and shoulders. Imagine that you are held in God's gentle, loving hands. Let yourself rest there and savor the quiet.

Pray for yourself. Focus on the light and warmth of God's love as it surrounds you. Rest in that light and warmth.

Bless me, God, with your love.

Bless me with your healing.

Bless me with your peace.

(Take a moment for several slow, deep breaths.)

Pray for a good friend. Bring them to mind as vividly as you are able. With this image, hold them in your heart, and extend love and grace to them. Now imagine them in God's gentle, loving hands. Allow them to rest there in God's hands for a moment.

Bless them, God, with your love.

Bless them with your healing.

Bless them with your peace.

(Take several deep breaths.)

Pray for someone for whom you do not have strong feelings. This may be an acquaintance you cross paths with on occasion but don't know well.

Bless them, God, with your love.

Bless them with your healing.

Bless them with your peace.

(Take several deep breaths.)

Pray for someone you dislike—an enemy. Imagine them in God's loving hands, and try to hold them gently in your heart. Release to God any anger or tension that may arise in you. Let these feelings go by setting them free to God's care.

Bless them, God, with your love.

Bless them with your healing.

Bless them with your peace.

(Take several deep breaths.)

Finally, pray for all four people together—yourself, a friend, an acquaintance, and an enemy. Extend God's blessing further—to everyone around you, to everyone in your neighborhood, to those in your town, and eventually to all people, everywhere. Imagine that we all are held in God's hands and sustained by God's love.

Bless all people, everywhere, with your love.

Bless all people with your healing.

Bless all people with your peace.

(Take several deep breaths, and bring your attention back to the present moment. Say a word of thanks to the Creator for this time.)

Day 29

Jesus offers a spiritual path that cultivates [radical] compassion. Many times compassion comes easily and naturally, like a child seeing a wounded bird and spontaneously tending to its broken wing. When whole and vital, our hearts automatically beat with care and connection. Often, however, much less sympathetic impulses drive our lives. The pulse of our spirit accelerates with drivenness or hyper-reactivity, it shuts down and dulls with numbness or fatigue, and it beats erratically in cycles of rage and withdrawal or compulsion and shame. Sometimes, compassion requires cultivation—the pulse of our lives feels off, it beats out of sync with the pulse of God's love, and it requires restoration to the tender heartbeat of care. At such times, the spiritual path of Jesus offers us a way to realign ourselves with God, to restore the pulse of our spirit, and to resuscitate and sustain our God-given capacities to embody care in the world. This spiritual path contains four rhythmic movements that transform the depleted or hardened heart to beat once more in harmony with the loving heartbeat of God. This fourfold rhythm entails deepening our connection with the expansive compassion of God, cultivating a self-compassion that recalibrates our erratic pulse to the steady pulse of our restored humanity, cultivating a compassion for the suffering that afflicts someone's humanity, and responding with concrete acts of embodied care and connection.

—Frank Rogers Jr., *Compassion in Practice*

Scripture

The Lord GOD has given me
    the tongue of a teacher,
that I may know how to sustain
    the weary with a word.
Morning by morning [the Lord GOD] wakens—
    wakens my ear
    to listen as those who are taught.
The Lord GOD has opened my ear,
    and I was not rebellious,
    I did not turn backward.
I gave my back to those who struck me,
    and my cheeks to those who pulled out the beard;
I did not hide my face
    from insult and spitting.

The Lord GOD helps me.

—Isaiah 50:4-7

Reflection

Sometimes, compassion does not come easily. In wilderness times, when hearts, minds, and spirits are overwhelmed with anxiety and sorrow, disasters and injustices, we may find it difficult to maintain compassion. We become numb to what is going on around us. Some call it "compassion fatigue."

At these times, we need compassion for ourselves. We cannot offer kindness to others if we ignore our own state of mind and heart. When we are overwhelmed or numbed out from all the suffering in the world, we need restoration. We may need to stop watching or listening to the news for a while. We can take breaks and carve out time for solitude and silence. We can engage in activities such as rest and recreation—undertakings that restore our hearts.

Holy One, help me when I become overwhelmed with the hurts and needs of my life and of the world. Restore my heart, mind, and spirit that I may be a follower who offers your compassionate heart to those around me. Amen.

Carry This Word in Your Heart Today

Restoration

Day 30

God has no favorites. Remember that scripture says, "For God so loved the *world*." Let us begin to see beyond race, beyond culture, beyond gender, beyond sexual orientation, beyond religion, beyond all these externals and see each other as God's beloved. When we relate to others as God relates to us, our sense of being God's beloved deepens even more.

—Trevor Hudson and Stephen D. Bryant,
The Way of Transforming Discipleship

Scripture

O give thanks to the LORD, for [the LORD] is good;
    [God's] steadfast love endures forever!
Let Israel say,
    "[God's] steadfast love endures forever." . . .

Open to me the gates of righteousness,
    that I may enter through them
    and give thanks to the LORD.

This is the gate of the LORD;
    the righteous shall enter through it.

I thank you that you have answered me
    and have become my salvation.

—Psalm 118:1-2, 19-21

Reflection

What a radical notion that "God has no favorites." In this season of wilderness, the message shouted by leaders and nations is often the opposite. We live in a world where hatred of *the other* is growing, a world where the income gap between rich and poor is increasing. Xenophobia declares its hatred in the light of day. Conflict escalates between people of different religions. People of color, undocumented immigrants, and those in the LGBTQIA+ community live in vulnerability. And the God of love calls us to proclaim the belovedness of all.

I confess that I frequently fall short in proclaiming that all are beloved. In the unsettledness of our current culture, I judge those who do not see the world the same way that I do. I struggle to understand the vastly different worldviews that are held by my fellow human beings. I frequently judge that I am right and that others are wrong.

Yet the God of creation calls me to see the belovedness of each person, to see that all people are held in the loving heart of God.

Holy One, I confess that I often do not see that you have no favorites. Help me to see others through your eyes, to relate to others as you relate to all of creation. We are all your beloved. Amen.

Carry This Word in Your Heart Today

Confession

Day 31

My prayer is simple:
May we choose love, Lord.
May we choose love when faced with retaliation,
love when tempted by deception,
love when addressing poverty,
love when speaking to our neighbors,
love when lured by bad choices,
love when electing leaders.
In all the things we do, in all the words we say, and in all the
    places we go,
may we always choose love.
Amen.

—Ciona D. Rouse, *Like Breath and Water:*
Praying with Africa

Scripture

When [Jesus] had come near Bethphage and Bethany, at the place called the Mount of Olives, he sent two of the disciples, saying, "Go into the village ahead of you, and as you enter it you will find tied there a colt that has never been ridden. Untie it and bring it here. If anyone asks you, 'Why are you untying it?' just say this, 'The Lord needs it.'"

—Luke 19:29-31

Reflection

As we begin to turn our attention toward Palm Sunday and the events of Holy Week, we read the scripture in which Jesus sends two of his disciples to find a colt that has never been ridden. This teacher, beloved of God, chooses love and calls us to follow that same path.

What does it mean for us to always choose love? When we choose love, we take care of the body, mind, and spirit that we have been given. We nourish our bodies with good food, exercise, and rest. We nourish our minds and spirits with prayer and meditation.

When we choose love, we see others as beloved children of God. We let go of judgment and cynicism. We assume the best intention of others.

When we choose love, we work for justice in the world. We acknowledge our privilege and work on our own prejudices. We confess that we are blind to many of our own biases and become ready to be transformed by God's spirit of love.

When we choose love, we look for God's face in the other, especially those we see as our enemies.

God of all creation, you created the world in love. Guide my steps and transform me into one who is able to choose love in all my endeavors. Amen.

Carry This Word in Your Heart Today

Love

Day 32

Following Jesus does not mean imitating Jesus, copying his way of doing things. If we imitate someone, we are not developing an intimate relationship with that person. Instead, following Jesus means to give our own unique form, our own unique incarnation, to God's love. To follow Jesus means to live our lives as authentically as he lived his. It means to give away our ego and follow the God of love as Jesus shows us how to do it. Loving our enemies is the core of the Christian message and the challenge that Jesus presents us. If we want to know what Jesus is about, and what following Jesus . . . is about, then the call to love our enemies is as close to the center as we can get.

—Henri J. M. Nouwen, *A Spirituality of Homecoming*

Scripture

Let the same mind be in you that was in Christ Jesus,
>   who, though he was in the form of God,
>   did not regard equality with God
>   as something to be exploited,
>   but emptied himself,
>   taking the form of a slave,
>   being born in human likeness.
>   And being found in human form,

he humbled himself
and became obedient to the point of death—
even death on a cross.

—Philippians 2:5-8

Reflection

I love these words from Henri J. M. Nouwen: "Following Jesus means to give . . . our own unique incarnation, to God's love." We don't "copy Jesus" but live authentically the best way we know how. Nouwen continues, "The call to love our enemies is as close to [Jesus' calling] as we can get."

And what a challenging calling, to love our enemies. It's easy for me to love my friends, my family, my coworkers, my pets. Loving my enemies—especially those I believe are harming me or those I love—is a nearly impossible task.

In these days of polarization, loving my enemies is not something I *want* to do. Some days, the best I can do is to pray for the willingness to pray for my enemies.

God of love, you ask that we love our enemies. If I can't love my enemies today, please help me be willing to pray for them. Today, may my enemies know love. Amen.

Carry This Word in Your Heart Today

Willingness

Day 33

Following Jesus is risky. We probably will have to step out of our comfort zones. And loving the world with God is iffy business. We will face frustrations, questions, and discouragement. What if we give our time and energy to others in need, but we don't see any results? What if we work hard for mercy and justice, and it doesn't seem to make a difference? What if we get up at four o'clock in the morning to provide breakfast at a shelter, and no one thanks us? . . . To put it plainly, taking risks for God's kingdom will frustrate and discourage us. But taking risks in response to God's love and the needs of others will change the world. Following Jesus into the world will challenge us emotionally, physically, relationally, and spiritually. We're likely to feel overwhelmed or even disillusioned. We may feel inadequate or ill-equipped. And we're right. We *will* be inadequate and ill-equipped if we forget that God works alongside us.

—Rebecca Dwight Bruff, *Loving the World with God*

Scripture

Be gracious to me, O Lord, for I am in distress;
   my eye wastes away from grief,
   my soul and body also.
For my life is spent with sorrow,

and my years with sighing;
my strength fails because of my misery,
    and my bones waste away.

I am the scorn of all my adversaries,
    a horror to my neighbors,
an object of dread to my acquaintances;
    those who see me in the street flee from me.
I have passed out of mind like one who is dead;
    I have become like a broken vessel.
For I hear the whispering of many—
    terror all around!—
as they scheme together against me,
    as they plot to take my life.

But I trust in you, O LORD;
    I say, "You are my God."
My times are in your hand;
    deliver me from the hand of my enemies and persecutors.
Let your face shine upon your servant;
    save me in your steadfast love."

—Psalm 31:9-16

Reflection

Jesus called the disciples to step outside their comfort zones. He called his followers to leave what was familiar and secure to follow him. Jesus challenges us to do the same: to give up the comfortable and familiar and follow him wherever he leads.

I live, most of the time, in a protective bubble, surrounded by friends, acquaintances, and colleagues who know me and love me just the way that I am. I am anxious about and resistant to the call to step outside of my comfort zone. But that is where I am called to go.

Taking risks for God's realm might mean working in an after-school tutoring program for children, having a conversation with someone who carries different political beliefs, or showing up at a rally to support political change. Taking risks for God's beloved ones may also mean speaking out for others when we have witnessed discrimination and hatred.

Give me courage, Holy One, to serve you even when it feels risky. Let me not forget that when I step outside my comfort zone, you are there. May I be transformed by your love. Amen.

Carry This Word in Your Heart Today

Transformation

Day 34

Living peaceably with everyone is difficult in a violent world. Daily we hear news reports of death and destruction that result from human greed and oppressive structures. Even Christians find it hard to overcome the desire to repay evil for evil. And yet that is what God calls us to do. We are called to bless and not curse those who do us harm; to strive for peace, leaving retributive justice to God; to show love at all times and in all places. . . . Living holy lives as Christians in the world demands that we hold fast to God if we intend to follow the path of love set by Christ. Living in harmony, even in the church, presents a challenge, as does showing hospitality to strangers, especially those who do not look like we do and whom we consider "other" because of difference in gender, race, class, sexuality, age, ability, or any other social definer. And yet that is God's call on our lives: to "leave peaceably with all." Living holy lives that demonstrate love requires that we acknowledge the *imago dei* (image of God) in each person and live actively in God's presence. By so doing we will be able to see and respond to their needs and seek justice for all.

—Gennifer Benjamin Brooks,
The Upper Room Disciplines 2017

Scripture

I thank you that you have answered me
    and have become my salvation.
The stone that the builders rejected
    has become the chief cornerstone.
This is the LORD's doing;
    it is marvelous in our eyes.
This is the day that the LORD has made;
    let us rejoice and be glad in it.
Save us, we beseech you, O LORD!
    O LORD, we beseech you, give us success!

Blessed is the one who comes in the name of the LORD.
    We bless you from the house of the LORD.
The LORD is God,
    and . . . has given us light.
Bind the festal procession with branches,
    up to the horns of the altar.

You are my God, and I will give thanks to you;
    you are my God, I will extol you.

O give thanks to the LORD, for [God] is good,
    for [the LORD's] steadfast love endures forever.

                      —Psalm 118:21-29

Reflection

On this eve of Holy Week, we think ahead to the events that will unfold before us. We walk through these days with Jesus and the disciples. We know about the songs of "Hosanna!" and the cries of "Crucify him!" We anticipate the meal where there will be both blessings and betrayals. We think about the cross and the pain, despair, and helplessness of the disciples.

We are called to live holy lives, to see God in each person, to show hospitality to all, to live peacefully with our neighbors and all God's creation,

Holy One, give me a heart of hospitality and eyes to see you in everyone I meet this day. Amen.

Carry This Word in Your Heart Today

Hospitality

Sixth Sunday in Lent

PALM/PASSION SUNDAY: HOSPITALITY

> All guests who present themselves are to be welcomed as Christ, for he himself will say: "I was a stranger and you welcomed me."
>
> —Benedict of Nursia (c. 480–547),
> *The Rule of St. Benedict*

Hospitality is a cornerstone of our spiritual ancestors. "You shall . . . love the stranger, for you were strangers in the land of Egypt" (Deut. 10:19). Providing hospitality for foreigners, food and clothing for the poor, protection for travelers—all these values were written in the laws of the Hebrew people. Because our faith is rooted in hospitality, it becomes even more upsetting when leaders of our countries have begun to legislate exclusion, the closing of borders, the mistreatment of migrants and refugees.

We live in a culture that fosters suspicion and hatred toward those who are different. What does it mean for us to live in an attitude of hospitality? It might mean welcoming someone different from us into our community or home. It might mean welcoming thoughts and feelings that we don't want to have and letting the Holy One transform them.

Motivated by fear or judgment, we struggle to welcome those who are different than we are. We see this in our nations and around the world as countries target immigrants and refugees with hatred and discrimination. We see this in our faith communities as they struggle over welcoming those who have a different sexual createdness into full participation in the ministries of the church.

We separate ourselves from one another through labels: rich/poor; Christian/non-Christian; conservative/liberal; straight/LGBTQIA+; citizen/undocumented; person of color/white; young/old. Yet we follow the one who broke down barriers of law, gender, class, and race, proclaiming a love that transcends all divisions. How do we live into that transcendent love in our daily lives?

Peter Storey, a leader in the South African Methodist Church's anti-apartheid movement, said when we open our hearts to Jesus, it's not just Jesus that we welcome. Jesus brings his friends—the neighbor whose political persuasion is opposite ours, the friend who is unhoused, the gay or lesbian teenager. Jesus says to us, "Love me, love my friends!"[1]

Loving God, enter my heart. Remove from me the rigidity of judgment, the fear that erects barriers, the need for control, the desire for others to be more like me. Give me a heart of hospitality, full of warmth, generosity, and acceptance. I am yours, gentle God. Amen.

Welcoming the Unwelcome into Our Hearts

Contemplative Outreach is an ecumenical organization created to support the practice of Centering Prayer as developed by Father Thomas Keating. Mary Mrozowski, one of the founders of Contemplative Outreach, created a prayer method called "The Welcoming Prayer." The Welcoming Prayer helps us make space in our hearts for any feeling or situation, whether positive or negative.

In the first movement of the prayer, you simply breathe while noticing the feeling in your body and your emotions.

In the second part of the prayer, you welcome whatever you are experiencing.

In the last part of the prayer, you let go of whatever you are experiencing by saying, "I let go of my desire for security, affection, control and embrace this moment as it is."[2]

Practice the Welcoming Prayer during everyday occurrences in your life—when you are stuck in traffic, when you are waiting at a doctor's office, when you have a few minutes in between meetings—so that you will be prepared to pray during more difficult times as well.

Guided Meditation on Hospitality

1. Close your eyes. Breathe in and out slowly three times.
2. You hear a knock on the door of your house. See yourself going quickly to answer it. Without hesitation, opening the door and inviting whoever or whatever is there to come in. Who is your guest? What is your guest doing and saying? Sense and feel how you are welcoming to your guest, even if he or she is not expected or acceptable to you.
3. Breathe in and out slowly three times.
4. See yourself sitting at your dinner table with all the seats being filled by strangers—people and other beings. Imagine that you are eating your meal. As you eat, you hear these words: "My child, you are entertaining angels." What happens next and how do you feel?
5. Breathe in and out slowly three times.
6. When you are ready, open your eyes. Take some time to pray or journal. Thank God for this experience of hospitality.

People who extend compassion to us are guardians of our soul. . . . These are people who see us, understand us, value us, and celebrate our homecomings. They offer us the inestimable gift of revealing to us the truth of who we are—we are worthy of love even in our shame; we are held with love even when we forget it; our beauty is beheld even when we feel blemished; though our journeys leave us broken and burdened, we are and remain thoroughly beloved.

—Frank Rogers Jr., *Practicing Compassion*

Scripture

Six days before the Passover Jesus came to Bethany, the home of Lazarus, whom he had raised from the dead. There they gave a dinner for him. Martha served, and Lazarus was one of those at the table with him. Mary took a pound of costly perfume made of pure nard, anointed Jesus' feet, and wiped them with her hair. The house was filled with the fragrance of the perfume.

—John 12:1-3

Reflection

In this scripture passage, Mary extends compassion to Jesus and, in this moment, anoints him with extravagant love. Who are the people in your life who have loved you unconditionally? Who have extended compassion to you even on your nastiest day? Who are the friends and family members who offer you hope when you are hopeless, who offer you love when you feel unlovable?

Keep watch today for friends and strangers who offer love in a challenging world. Be alert to those situations where you can be an emissary of love for a person who needs to be reminded that they are beloved.

God of love, this world is a broken place. Send me to those people and places where your love and compassion are needed. Amen.

Carry This Word in Your Heart Today

Compassion

Day 36

In this world's eyes, there is an enormous distinction between good times and bad, between sorrow and joy. But in the eyes of God, they are never separated. Our ministry is to help people gradually let go of their resentment and discover that right in the middle of suffering there is a blessing. Where there is pain, there is healing. Where there is mourning, there is dancing. Where there is poverty, there is the Kingdom of God. Jesus says to us, "Cry over your pains, and you will discover that I'm right there in your tears, and you will be grateful for my presence in your weakness."

—Henri J. M. Nouwen, *A Spirituality of Living*

Scripture

"Very truly, I tell you, unless a grain of wheat falls into the earth and dies, it remains just a single grain; but if it dies, it bears much fruit. Those who love their life lose it, and those who hate their life in this world will keep it for eternal life. Whoever serves me must follow me, and where I am, there will my servant be also. Whoever serves me, the Father will honor."

—John 12:24-26

Reflection

Recently I had the honor of sitting with a church friend and her family during the last week of her life. Such a difficult, beautiful, blessed experience to be there in those days when minutes seem to slow down to the pace of breaths and every little word or smile or touch is burned into memory.

And God was right there in the pain and in the grief and in the tears. God was right there in the last breaths and in the love shared. God was right there in the empty place left after the funeral home took the loved one's body away. God was right there through the memorial service in the memories and the stories, in the scriptures and the hymns, in the love shared amongst friends and family and neighbors.

God of life, you are right there with me in my most painful moments. I am grateful for your presence. Amen.

———

Carry This Word in Your Heart Today

Blessing

Carry a little quiet inside you
while the world continues
in rush and rage
fighting and frenzy.

Carry a little quiet inside you
so that the worry and war
trouble and tumult
do not capture you in their grip

Tarry in the Son-filled meadow of the heart
beside the still waters
where God's Spirit refreshes and renews

Carry so much quiet inside you
that you have some extra calm
to share with me.
　　　—Safiyah Fosua, *The Africana Worship Book: Year A*

Scripture

Jesus was troubled in spirit, and declared, "Very truly, I tell you, one of you will betray me." The disciples looked at one another, uncertain of whom he was speaking. One of his disciples—the one whom Jesus loved—was reclining next to him; Simon Peter therefore motioned to him to ask Jesus of whom he was speaking. So while reclining next to Jesus, he asked him,

"Lord, who is it?" Jesus answered, "It is the one to whom I give this piece of bread when I have dipped it in the dish." So when he had dipped the piece of bread, he gave it to Judas son of Simon Iscariot.

—John 13:21-26

Reflection

Jesus—divine *and* human—felt the same sorrow and distress that we would feel by a betrayal. For three years, he had poured his life into the disciples, eating, sleeping, walking, and living with them. And Jesus knew that Judas would betray him.

As we walk with Jesus through this Holy Week, may we consider the very human emotions that Jesus experienced, along with times when we have experienced betrayal in our own lives. When betrayal comes from a trusted friend, the wound is so much more painful.

How did Jesus make it through this week of betrayal, heartbreak, and suffering? We know he found a quiet place to pray, as he had done during his years of ministry. Today, may we find a quiet place today and open our hearts to prayer.

Holy One, I have been both the betrayed and the betrayer. Forgive me for my moments of faithlessness. Heal my wounds and give me a heart of forgiveness. May I find a quiet place with you today. Amen.

Carry This Word in Your Heart Today

Betrayal

Day 38

MAUNDY THURSDAY

At the deepest levels, what takes place during the Holy Meal? What life-transforming dynamic occurs when your congregation celebrates the Lord's Supper? Perhaps we can helpfully imagine the Eucharist as spending time in "sorrow's kitchen." . . . In sorrow's kitchen we mix the ingredients of our passage from death to life. We take, bless, break, and give the bread that is moistened with the world's tears, including our own. We add the flour of grain crushed and pulverized by the millstone of oppression, grief, and neglect. In other words, grateful celebration of the Eucharist finds a way to include and declare truthfully that life hurts. Passage from death to life, from sin to love, from living in the dark to living in the light, is painful. . . . The Eucharist is "sorrow's kitchen" because it is where death and life meet each week.

—Daniel T. Benedict Jr., *Patterned by Grace*

Scripture

"I give you a new commandment, that you love one another. Just as I have loved you, you also should love one another. By this everyone will know that you are my disciples, if you have love for one another."

—John 13:34-35

Reflection

I worship each week at a small, inner-city church. Founded in 1965 as one of the first interracial congregations in Tennessee, it was created as a place where all people are welcome. From the beginning, the founding members shared the Holy Meal together each week. They needed the sustenance that came from that regular gathering, blessing, breaking, and sharing.

Over the years, the members of this congregation have been contemplatives and activists, persons of all ages, races, sexual orientations, gender identities, nations, and economic situations. At this holy meal where Christ is the host, the congregation affirms each week, "Everyone has a place at this table."

The Holy Meal is a come-as-you-are occasion. We can bring our tears and our sorrows, our mistakes and our shortcomings. We can bring our hopes for the world and our despair over its brokenness. At the table that Christ sets before us, sorrow and laughter meet and sit side-by-side.

Holy One, you set an abundant table of love before me. Let me love others as you have loved me. Amen.

Carry This Word in Your Heart Today

Sorrow

Day 39

GOOD FRIDAY

Into the compassionate Womb of your love, O God,
 I bring my deepest needs, my strongest hopes, my
  greatest fears.

Give me tears for my grief, a voice that I might cry out to
 you.
Give me words that I might say what is most on my heart.
Give me courage, so that I will always seek the healing you
 have to give.
Let me always offer my suffering to you,
 So that when healing does not come,
  Wisdom, justice, and compassion may be its fruit,
   a life given to you,
   Abba God. Amen.
    —Jerry P. Haas, *The Upper Room Worshipbook*

Scripture

They took Jesus; and carrying the cross by himself, he went out to what is called The Place of the Skull, which in Hebrew is called Golgotha. There they crucified him, and with him two others, one on either side, with Jesus between them.

            —John 19:16-18

Reflection

Today is Good Friday, the most solemn day in the liturgical year. Some-times I find myself dreading this day. And yet we walk this path with Jesus every year, and every year we arrive at Good Friday and the cru-cifixion of Jesus.

It is challenging to confront the reality of death, of human fail-ings, of evil. Perhaps, this yearly opportunity is the gift of Good Friday. Death, human failings, and evil surround us at all times. But in this holy narrative, Jesus' death is not the end. The end of the story is God's victory over death, over evil, over all the hatred and prejudice the world can summon.

This is our hope in these days of wilderness. The poverty, hatred, injustice, and prejudice that we see around us are not the end. God is working on behalf of the least of these. And when it seems that evil prevails, we know that God's presence is with us and with all those who suffer. We are not alone. Our God walks with us, sits and weeps with us, holds us in our anguish and in our death, and offers us new life.

Holy One, I stand before you on this day of sorrow. Let me be your presence with those who are struggling, grieving, in despair. May I be love to them. Amen.

Carry This Word in Your Heart Today

Death

Day 40

HOLY SATURDAY

We cannot escape waiting. Such is life. We are always waiting. What can we learn from this truth that all would prefer not to have to endure? On the one hand, it encourages us to pay attention. It reminds us that we need to "Be still, and know that I am God" (Ps. 46:10). In so doing, we learn to see through the eyes of discernment. Above all, waiting can teach us that God's love will lead us. A mutual relationship with God will lead us to green pastures and wells of abundant grace that anoint us with God's unending provision and love.

—Marysol Diaz, *The Upper Room Disciplines 2017*

Scripture

[Joseph of Arimathea] went to Pilate and asked for the body of Jesus; then Pilate ordered it to be given to him. So Joseph took the body and wrapped it in a clean linen cloth and laid it in his own new tomb, which he had hewn in the rock. He then rolled a great stone to the door of the tomb and went away. Mary Magdalene and the other Mary were there, sitting opposite the tomb.

—Matthew 27:58-61

Reflection

This was the day that the women waited. Jesus' body was taken to the tomb of Joseph of Arimathea. But because the sabbath began at sundown, they could not do the work of preparing the body for burial. So they waited. They waited in fear, in sorrow, in numbness. The dreams that they held had died on the cross with their beloved teacher.

Sometimes we wait in joyful anticipation. For the birth of a new baby, for a family celebration, for retirement or a birthday. Other times, we wait in fear or dread. And this type of waiting is especially difficult. Yet we continue to wait. We hold our collective breath as we wait. For a death, for the results of a biopsy, for an email after a job interview.

Whether we wait in hope or in dread, we are not alone.

For those who wait in despair, in grief, in sorrow. For those who wait in the paths of storms, in detention camps, in hospice rooms. For those who wait in tender hope, in tear-streaked sadness, in fearful anticipation. Bless, Loving Healer, all those who wait. For you are their comfort. You are their strength. Amen.

Carry This Word in Your Heart Today

Wait

Easter

The strongest evidence for the Resurrection is the transformed lives of Jesus' disciples. How else do we explain the sudden transformation that took place in their lives? Within days those frightened and grieving disciples are transformed into bold and courageous witnesses willing to die for their faith. Something most extraordinary must have taken place for this to have happened. The One whom they follow is raised from the grave, and they encounter him in a way that convinces them he is now living beyond crucifixion. The Resurrection means much for our lives today. Christ is present with us as our loving Friend. He is available to each one of us in our struggle with the forces of evil. We too can experience "little Easters" in the midst of those things that make us "die" each day—the betrayal of a friend, the cruelty of a colleague, or even the failure of a dream. Easter reminds us that the risen Christ always can bring light and life where we see only darkness and death.

—Trevor Hudson, *Pauses for Lent*

Scripture

Early on the first day of the week, while it was still dark, Mary Magdalene came to the tomb and saw that the stone had been removed from the tomb. So she ran and went to Simon Peter and the other disciple, the one whom Jesus loved, and said to them, "They have taken the Lord out of the tomb, and we do not know where they have laid him."

—John 20:1-2

Reflection

What a life-changing morning for Mary Magdalene and the other disciples. Arriving at the tomb to prepare Jesus' body, she found the tomb open and Jesus' body missing. "I have seen the Lord," she tells the other disciples (John 20:18). Christ, though crucified, was alive and present with grieving disciples.

The risen Christ is our companion today in these times of wilderness. Christ is present with people in jails and prisons. Christ is present with the sick, the dying, and those who mourn. Christ is present with young and old who march in the streets, calling for justice for Black lives. Christ is present with migrants all over the world who are fleeing violence and poverty.

Christ stands with us as we face the challenges of growing old, as we struggle with the death of a loved one, as we stand face to face with injustice and evil. Christ calls our name, and we recognize his presence with us.

Holy One, you are present with us in our sorrow and despair, our joy and our hope. May I recognize you and call you friend. Amen.

Carry This Word in Your Heart Today

Friend

Small-Group Guide

Follow this outline for six one-hour gatherings to study the book during the season of Lent. You may have one designated leader or may rotate the leadership among the participants. If possible, gather in a comfortable place. You'll only need your books and a candle that can be lit at the beginning of each session.

Format for the Sessions

Opening (1 minute)

Leader: God be with you.
People: And also with you.
Leader: We light this candle to signify that God is present.
People: Holy One, we thank you for your presence in this place.

Reading (5 minutes)

The leader reads a quote, a scripture, or a reflection from among the days of this week. (Pick a selection that stands out because of its resonance in your life or because it challenged you.) Spend a few minutes in silence after the reading.

Responding (20 minutes)

Invite participants to share what they heard in the reading or how God has spoken to them from what they have read.

Practicing (20 minutes)

Name the practice that was shared in the Sunday reflection. Ask the group members what they have learned by reading or engaging in the practice. If you have time, walk through the practice together.

Closing (10 minutes)

Before you leave, share prayer concerns with one another. The leader or a participant can close the group with prayer.

Group Guidelines[1]

This group will encourage and provide mutual support for individual journeys through the Lenten season. Participants agree to meet weekly during the season of Lent and come prepared to the group sessions. The leader will assure that the group will start and end on time. Participants agree as follows:

- To be present at every session. If unable to attend, alert the leader so group members can continue to support you in your absence.
- Respect what other people say. Share from your own experience. Don't give advice or try to fix another person. Honor another person's experience by listening deeply and not focusing your mind on what you will say next.
- Give others time to share. Be sensitive to the amount of time you speak, and make sure that others have time also. At the same time, know that sharing in the group is not mandatory. If someone does not wish to say anything, please respect that person's desire.
- Observe confidentiality. What others talk about in the group stays in the group.
- Don't fear the silence. If no one has anything to say, rest in the quiet. God can speak through the silence. Participants may want to exchange phone numbers or email addresses to be in touch with one another for support during the coming weeks.

Litanies for Worship

Use these litanies during the corporate worship time at your church or during your personal or small-group devotional time on Ash Wednesday or during Holy Week. These litanies are based on the scripture passages from the Revised Common Lectionary, Year B.

Permission is granted to use these litanies in corporate worship. If prayers are reproduced, please add the following credit line: From *Walking in the Wilderness: Seeking God During Lent* by Beth A. Richardson. Copyright © 2020. Used by permission of Upper Room Books. For more information, visit upperroombooks.com.

Ash Wednesday

Leader: We come to this day of ashes, and we are in a wilderness. Our hearts are troubled. Our people are fighting. Our earth is crying.

People: Even now, says the LORD, return to me with all your heart, with fasting, with weeping, and with mourning.

Leader: You call us to follow you into this season of repentance and preparation, but we are an anxious, distracted people.

People: Even now, says the LORD, return to me with all your heart, with fasting, with weeping, and with mourning.

Leader: Guide us as we follow the path of Jesus and his disciples as they walked toward Jerusalem.

People: Even now, says the LORD, return to me with all your heart, with fasting, with weeping, and with mourning.

Leader: Fill our hearts with you as we offer alms, as we pray, as we fast.

People: Even now, says the LORD, return to me with all your heart, with fasting, with weeping, and with mourning.

Leader: Journey with us through this season that we might know and love you more deeply. That you might mark our lives even as we receive this mark of ashes.

People: Even now, says the LORD, return to me with all your heart, with fasting, with weeping, and with mourning. Amen.

*Based on Joel 2:1-2, 12-17 and Matthew 6:1-6, 16-21

Palm Sunday

Leader: The people are gathering: young and old, rich and poor, peasant and lord. All cry:

People: Hosanna! Blessed is the one who comes in the name of the Lord!

Leader: Someone is coming. He rides on a colt.

People: Hosanna! Blessed is the one who comes in the name of the Lord!

Leader: Palm branches and cloaks cover the road to Jerusalem.

People: Hosanna! Blessed is the one who comes in the name of the Lord!

Leader: Who is this one? He is God's beloved.

People: Hosanna! Blessed is the one who comes in the name of the Lord!

Leader: We are gathering too: young and old, rich and poor, every gender, every hue, we cry:

People: Hosanna! Blessed is the one who comes in the name of the Lord! Amen.

*Based on Mark 11:1-11

Maundy Thursday

Leader: Today we gather around Christ's table, the table of love. You commanded us,

People: "Just as I have loved you, you also should love one another."

Leader: We acknowledge the brokenness of ourselves, our communities, our world. You invite us,

People: "Just as I have loved you, you also should love one another."

Leader: Around this table, your disciples gathered. Men and women, followers of you. You said to them,

People: "Just as I have loved you, you also should love one another."

Leader: You took a towel and basin and, like a servant, washed everyone's feet, saying,

People: "Just as I have loved you, you also should love one another."

Leader: Today we break the bread and lift the cup, reminding us of you, reminding us that you said,

People: "Just as I have loved you, you also should love one another."

Leader: May we live this commandment in our lives, in our communities, in our world.

People: "Just as I have loved you, you also should love one another." Amen.

*Based on John 13:1-17, 31-35

Good Friday

Leader: On this day, Jesus was hung on a cross in a place called Golgotha.

People: But we trust in you, O LORD; and say, "You are our God."

Leader: On this day, the sky turned black in the middle of the day.

People: But we trust in you, O LORD; and say, "You are our God."

Leader: On this day, Jesus called out, "My God, my God, why have you forsaken me?"

People: But we trust in you, O Lord; and say, "You are our God."

Leader: On this day, Jesus gave a loud cry and breathed his last breath.

People: But we trust in you, O Lord; and say, "You are our God."

Leader: On this day, the women stood witness.

People: But we trust in you, O Lord; and say, "You are our God."

Leader: On this day, Love was crucified.

People: But we trust in you, O Lord; and say, "You are our God." Amen.

*Based on Psalm 31:9-16 and Mark 15:1-39

Holy Saturday

Leader: After these things, Joseph of Arimathea, who was a disciple of Jesus, asked Pilate to let him take away the body of Jesus.

People: In you, O Lord, I seek refuge; in your righteousness deliver me.

Leader: Nicodemus also came, bringing a mixture of myrrh and aloes.

People: In you, O Lord, I seek refuge; in your righteousness deliver me.

Leader: They took the body of Jesus and wrapped it with the spices in linen cloths, according to the burial custom of the Jews.

People: In you, O Lord, I seek refuge; in your righteousness deliver me.

Leader: There was a garden in the place where Jesus was crucified, and in the garden there was a new tomb in which no one had ever been laid.

People: In you, O Lord, I seek refuge; in your righteousness deliver me.

Leader: And so, because it was the Jewish day of Preparation and the tomb was nearby, they laid Jesus there.

People: In you, O Lᴏʀᴅ, I seek refuge; in your righteousness deliver me. Amen.

*Based on Psalm 31:1-4, 15-16 and John 19:38-42

Easter

Leader: We have walked in the wilderness, never abandoned, never alone.

People: Christ is risen! Christ is risen, indeed!

Leader: We have followed the steps of Jesus with disciples and crowds on dusty roads.

People: Christ is risen! Christ is risen, indeed!

Leader: We have sat at table for the Passover meal and watched the betrayal.

People: Christ is risen! Christ is risen, indeed!

Leader: We have witnessed the trial, the crucifixion, the day of waiting.

People: Christ is risen! Christ is risen, indeed!

Leader: And now the tomb is empty.

People: Christ is risen! Christ is risen, indeed!

Leader: Death has been conquered by love, and we are never abandoned, never alone.

People: Christ is risen! Christ is risen, indeed! Amen.

*Based on John 20:1-18

Notes

Epigraph

Rueben P. Job, Norman Shawchuck, and John S. Mogabgab, *A Guide to Prayer for All Who Walk with God* (Nashville, TN: Upper Room Books, 2013), x.

Introduction

Epigraph. Saint Theophan the Recluse, *The Art of Prayer: An Orthodox Anthology*, comp. Igumen Chariton of Valamo, trans. E Kadloubovsky and E. M. Palmer, ed. Timothy Ware (London: Faber and Faber, 1966), 119.

1. David Rensberger, "Deserted Spaces," *Weavings: A Journal of the Christian Spiritual Life* 16, no. 3 (May/June 2001): 7, 12–13.

2. Phyllis Tickle, *Emergence Christianity: What It Is, Where It Is Going, and Why It Matters* (Grand Rapids, MI: Baker Books, 2012), 17.

3. Rensberger, "Deserted Spaces," 12.

4. Sarah Parsons, *A Clearing Season: Reflections for Lent* (Nashville, TN: Upper Room Books, 2005), 13.

5. This section is adapted from Beth A. Richardson's *The Uncluttered Heart: Making Room for God During Advent and Christmas* (Nashville: Upper Room Books, 2009), 13–15.

Day 1: Ash Wednesday

Epigraph. Juanita Campbell Rasmus, "Ash Wednesday," *Alive Now* 42, no. 2 (March/April 2012): 37.

Day 2

Epigraph. Sarah Parsons, *A Clearing Season: Reflections for Lent* (Nashville, TN: Upper Room Books, 2005), 13.

Day 3

Epigraph. George Hovaness Donigian, *A World Worth Saving: Lenten Spiritual Practices for Action* (Nashville, TN: Upper Room Books, 2013), 17–18, 23–24.

Day 4

Epigraph. Jane E. Vennard with Stephen D. Bryant, *The Way of Prayer: Participant's Book*, Companions in Christ (Nashville, TN: Upper Room Books, 2006), 77.

Day 5

Epigraph. L. Roger Owens, *What We Need Is Here: Practicing the Heart of Christian Spirituality* (Nashville, TN: Upper Room Books, 2015), 33.

Day 6

Epigraph. Jane Herring, *One Day I Wrote Back: Interacting with Scripture through Creative Writing* (Nashville, TN: Upper Room Books, 2015), 58–59.

Day 7

Epigraph. Pamela Hawkins, *Weavings: A Journal of the Christian Spiritual Life* 27, no. 2 (February/March/April 2011): 48.

Day 8

Epigraph. Roberta C. Bondi, *Wild Things: Poems of Grief and Love, Loss and Gratitude* (Nashville, TN: Upper Room Books, 2014), 19–20.

Day 9

Epigraph. Safiyah Fosua, "Collect Our Tears," *The Africana Worship Book: Year B*, ed. Valerie Bridgman David and Safiyah Fosua (Nashville, TN: Discipleship Resources, 2007), 178.

Day 10

Epigraph. Rueben P. Job, Norman Shawchuck, and John S. Mogabgab, *A Guide to Prayer for All Who Walk with God* (Nashville, TN: Upper Room Books, 2013), 151.

Day 11

Epigraph. Elizabeth J. Canham, *Finding Your Voice in the Psalms: An Invitation to Honest Prayer* (Nashville, TN: Upper Room Books, 2013), 56.

Day 12

Epigraph. Flora Slosson Wuellner, *Miracle: When Christ Touches Our Deepest Need* (Nashville, TN: Upper Room Books, 2008), 82–83.

Day 13

Epigraph. Michael W. Waters, *Freestyle: Reflections on Faith, Family, Justice, and Pop Culture* (Nashville, TN: Fresh Air Books, 2014), 138.

Day 14

Epigraph. Christopher Maricle, *Deeply Rooted: Knowing Self, Growing in God* (Nashville, TN: Upper Room Books, 2016), 45–46.

Day 15

Epigraph. Junius Dotson, "True Intimacy," *The Africana Worship Book: Year C*, ed. Valerie Bridgeman Davis and Safiyah Fosua (Nashville, TN: Discipleship Resources, 2008), 41.

Day 16

Epigraph. Irenaeus, "Psalm Prayer (Ps. 139)," *Upper Room Worshipbook: Music and Liturgies for Spiritual Formation*, ed. Elise S. Eslinger (Nashville, TN: Upper Room Books, 2006), 348.

Third Sunday in Lent: *Lectio Divina*

1. Origen, "Letter of Origen to Gregory," *The Fathers of the Church: St. Gregory Thaumaturgus, Life and Works*, trans. Michael Slusser (Washington, DC: The Catholic University of America Press, 1998), 192.

Day 17

Epigraph. George Hovaness Donigian, *A World Worth Saving: Lenten Spiritual Practices for Action* (Nashville, TN: Upper Room Books, 2013), 105.

Day 18

Epigraph. Michael W. Waters, *Freestyle: Reflections on Faith, Family, Justice, and Pop Culture* (Nashville, TN: Fresh Air Books, 2014), 76.

1. Richard Rohr, "The Sacred Wound," Center for Action and Contemplation, October 16, 2015, https://cac.org/the-sacred-wound-2015-10-16/.

Day 19

Epigraph. Trevor Hudson, *Invitations of Jesus* (Nashville, TN: Upper Room Books, 2014), 24.

Day 20

Epigraph. Evelyn Underhill, *Writings of Evelyn Underhill*, Upper Room Spiritual Classics, ed. Keith Beasley-Topliffe (Nashville, TN: Upper Room Books, 1998), 37–38.

Day 21

Epigraph. John Mogabgab, "Editor's Introduction," *Weavings: A Journal of the Christian Spiritual Life* 24, no. 3 (May/June 2009): 2.

Day 22

Epigraph. John R. Wimmer, *Blessed Endurance: Moving Beyond Despair to Hope* (Nashville, TN: Upper Room Books, 2017), 32.

Fourth Sunday in Lent: Trust

1. Daniel Wolpert, *Creating a Life with God: The Call of Ancient Prayer Practices* (Nashville, TN: Upper Room Books, 2003), 18.

Day 23

Epigraph. Julian of Norwich, *Writings of Julian of Norwich*, Upper Room Spiritual Classics, ed. Keith Beasley-Topliffe (Nashville, TN: Upper Room Books, 1998), 34.

Day 24

Epigraph. Elaine A. Heath, *God Unbound: Wisdom from Galatians for the Anxious Church* (Nashville, TN: Upper Room Books, 2016), 70–71.

Day 25

Epigraph. Thomas Porter, *The Spirit and Art of Conflict Transformation: Creating a Culture of* JustPeace (Nashville, TN: Upper Room Books, 2010), 28–29.

Day 26

Epigraph. Kwasi I. Kena, *The Africana Worship Book: Year A*, ed. Valerie Bridgeman Davis and Safiyah Fosua (Nashville, TN: Discipleship Resources, 2006), 156.

Day 27

Epigraph. Regina M. Laroche, "The Touch of Ashes," *Weavings: A Journal of the Christian Spiritual Life* 31, no. 2 (February/March/April 2016): 7–8.

Day 28

Epigraph. J. David Muyskens, *Sacred Breath: Forty Days of Centering Prayer* (Nashville, TN: Upper Room Books, 2010), 16.

Fifth Sunday in Lent: Compassion

1. Thich Nhat Hanh, *No Mud, No Lotus* (Berkeley, CA: Parallax Press, 2014), 104.
2. Kathleen Stephens, "A Blessing Exercise," The Upper Room, https://www.upperroom.org/resources/a-blessing-exercise.

Day 29

Epigraph. Frank Rogers Jr., *Compassion in Practice: The Way of Jesus* (Nashville, TN: Upper Room Books, 2016), 34–35.

Day 30

Epigraph. Trevor Hudson and Stephen D. Bryant, *The Way of Transforming Discipleship: Participant's Book*, Companions in Christ (Nashville, TN: Upper Room Books, 2005), 25.

Day 31

Epigraph. Ciona D. Rouse, *Like Breath and Water: Praying with Africa* (Nashville, TN: Upper Room Books, 2009), 61.

Day 32

Epigraph. Henri J. M. Nouwen, *A Spirituality of Homecoming,* The Henri Nouwen Spirituality Series, ed. John S. Mogabgab (Nashville, TN: Upper Room Books, 2012), 31.

Day 33

Epigraph. Rebecca Dwight Bruff, *Loving the World with God: Fourth Day Living* (Nashville, TN: Upper Room Books, 2014), 64–65.

Day 34

Epigraph. Gennifer Benjamin Brooks, "The Challenge in the Call," *The Upper Room Disciplines 2017* (Nashville, TN: Upper Room Books, 2016), 292.

Sixth Sunday in Lent: Palm/Passion Sunday, Hospitality

Epigraph. Benedict of Nursia, *The Rule of St. Benedict in English,* ed. Timothy Fry, OSB (Collegeville, MN: The Liturgical Press, 1981), 53:1.

1. Peter Storey, *Listening at Golgotha: Jesus' Words from the Cross* (Nashville, TN: Upper Room Books, 2004), 30.

2. "The Welcoming Prayer," Contemplative Outreach, https://www.contemplativeoutreach.org/sites/default/files/private/welcoming_prayer_trifold_2016.pdf.

Day 35

Epigraph. Frank Rogers Jr., *Practicing Compassion* (Nashville, TN: Fresh Air Books, 2015), 44.

Day 36

Epigraph. Henri J. M. Nouwen, *A Spirituality of Living,* The Henri Nouwen Spirituality Series, ed. John S. Mogabgab (Nashville, TN: Upper Room Books, 2011), 48.

Day 37

Epigraph. Safiyah Fosua, "Generous Quietude," *The Africana Worship Book: Year A,* ed. Valerie Bridgeman Davis and Safiyah Fosua (Nashville, TN: Discipleship Resources, 2006), 37.

Day 38: Maundy Thursday

Epigraph. Daniel T. Benedict Jr., *Patterned by Grace: How Liturgy Shapes Us* (Nashville, TN: Upper Room Books, 2007), 114–15.

Day 39: Good Friday

Epigraph. Jerry P. Haas, "A Prayer of Petition for Healing," *Upper Room Worshipbook: Music and Liturgies for Spiritual Formation,* ed. Elise S. Eslinger (Nashville, TN: Upper Room Books, 2006), 32.

Day 40: Holy Saturday

Epigraph. Marysol Diaz, "Trust in God's Leading," *The Upper Room Disciplines 2017* (Nashville, TN: Upper Room Books, 2016), 225.

Easter

Epigraph. Trevor Hudson, *Pauses for Lent: 40 Words for 40 Days* (Nashville, TN: Upper Room Books, 2015), 63.

Small-Group Guide

1. These guidelines are adapted from Beth A. Richardson's *The Uncluttered Heart: Making Room for God During Advent and Christmas* (Nashville, TN: Upper Room Books, 2009), 100.